P9-CRZ-301

Best of Country
Casseroles

Down-Home Cookbook Dishes Out Hearty Casseroles!

NOTHING hits the spot like hot and wholesome comfort food. That's why hearty casseroles are a tasty stand-by in kitchens across the country throughout the year.

Want to treat your family to delicious one-dish wonders the whole gang will favor? Turn to this *Best of Country Casseroles* cookbook! From beef, chicken and pork to seafood fare, meatless meals and breakfast casseroles, this special collection contains 221 dishes suited to meet your mealtime needs around the clock.

Taste buds will rise and take a shine to Sausage Egg Bake (p. 9), Hash Brown Casserole (p. 10) and Breakfast Bread Pudding (p. 14). For the midday meal, Grilled Cheese in a Pan (p. 85) and Sloppy Joe Under a Bun (p. 24) fit the bill. And your options for dinner are endless with such selections as Chicken Stir-Fry Bake (p. 43), Pork Chop Casserole (p. 58) and Fish Stick Supper (p. 70). Forty-four side-dish casseroles round out the robust lineup.

Fellow cooks from across the country shared these family-favorite recipes, which have appeared in past issues of *Taste of Home* magazine and its "sister" publications. Our home economists prepared and taste-tested them as well, compiling the most hearty, filling ones into this down-home collection.

So dig in to the *Best of Country Casseroles* cookbook…you'll love these one-dish meals!

Editor: Jean Steiner
Art Directors: Kathy Crawford, Catherine Fletcher
Executive Editor, Books: Heidi Reuter Lloyd
Associate Editor: Beth Wittlinger
Proofreader: Julie Blume
Food Editor: Janaan Cunningham
Associate Food Editors: Coleen Martin, Diane Werner
Senior Recipe Editor: Sue A. Jurack
Recipe Editor: Janet Briggs
Editorial Assistant: Barb Czysz
Food Photographers: Rob Hagen, Dan Roberts, Jim Wieland
Set Stylists: Julie Ferron, Stephanie Marchese,
Sue Myers, Jennifer Bradley Vent
Photographers Assistant: Lori Foy
Chairman and Founder: Roy Reiman
President: Barbara Newton
Senior Vice President, Editor in Chief: Catherine Cassidy

© 2005 Reiman Media Group, Inc.
5400 S. 60th St., Greendale WI 53129
International Standard Book Number: 0-89821-453-X
Library of Congress Control Number: 2005904130
All rights reserved. Printed in China.
Third Printing, April 2008

Pictured on Front Cover: Biscuit Pizza Bake (p. 24)

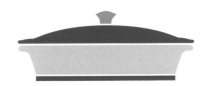

Table of Contents

Makes a Great Gift!

To order additional copies of this *Best of Country Casseroles* book, specify item number 35054 and send $15.99 (plus $4.95 shipping/insured delivery for one book, $5.50 for two or more) to: Country Store, Suite 7727, P.O. Box 990, Greendale WI 53129-0990. To order by credit card, call toll-free 1-800/558-1013 or visit our Web site at *www.reimanpub.com*.

Breakfast

Sausage Egg Bake, p. 9

Chapter 1

Zucchini Egg Bake

(Pictured below)

This wonderfully moist brunch dish can be made a day early and stored in the refrigerator to save time. Loaded with zucchini, herbs and cheese, it goes well with croissants and fresh fruit.
—*Kim Hafner, East Walpole, Massachusetts*

      3 cups chopped peeled zucchini
      1 large onion, chopped
      2 garlic cloves, minced
  1/4 cup butter
      4 eggs
  1/2 cup grated Parmesan cheese
  1/4 cup minced fresh parsley
1-1/2 teaspoons minced fresh basil *or* 1/2
      teaspoon dried basil
1-1/2 teaspoons minced fresh marjoram *or* 1/2
      teaspoon dried marjoram
  1/2 teaspoon salt
  1/2 cup shredded Monterey Jack cheese

In a large skillet, saute the zucchini, onion and garlic in butter until tender; set aside. In a large bowl, whisk the eggs, Parmesan cheese, parsley, basil, marjoram and salt. Stir in zucchini mixture and Monterey Jack cheese.

Pour into a greased 1-qt. baking dish. Bake at 350° for 20-25 minutes or until a knife inserted near the center comes out clean. Let stand for 5 minutes before serving. **Yield:** 6 servings.

Tex-Mex Cheese Strata

Tortilla chips add a little fun to this south-of-the-border brunch. For spicier tastes, substitute pepper Jack for the Monterey Jack cheese. —*Vickie Lowrey*
Fallon, Nevada

      4 cups coarsely crushed nacho tortilla
      chips
      2 cups (8 ounces) shredded Monterey
      Jack cheese
      1 small onion, finely chopped
      1 tablespoon butter
      6 eggs
2-1/2 cups milk
      1 can (4 ounces) chopped green chilies,
      undrained
      3 tablespoons ketchup
  1/4 teaspoon hot pepper sauce

Arrange tortilla chips in a greased 13-in. x 9-in. x 2-in. baking dish; sprinkle with cheese and set aside. In a skillet, saute onion in butter until tender. In a bowl, whisk the eggs, milk, onion, chilies, ketchup and hot pepper sauce; pour over cheese. Cover and refrigerate overnight.

Remove from the refrigerator 30 minutes before baking. Bake, uncovered, at 350° for 40-45 minutes or until a thermometer reads 160° and a knife inserted near the center comes out clean. Let stand for 5 minutes before cutting. **Yield:** 6-8 servings.

Individual Brunch Casseroles

I created this recipe one Sunday morning when I needed to use up some potatoes. —*Peggy Meador*
Kell, Illinois

      3 cups shredded uncooked potatoes
  3/4 cup diced onion
  1/2 cup diced celery
  1/2 cup diced green pepper
      2 to 4 tablespoons vegetable oil
      4 eggs
  1/2 teaspoon salt
  1/4 teaspoon pepper
      1 cup (4 ounces) shredded cheddar
      cheese
  1/2 pound sliced bacon, cooked and
      crumbled

1 can (4 ounces) mushroom stems and pieces, drained

In a large skillet, saute the potatoes, onion, celery and green pepper in 2 tablespoons oil until vegetables are tender, adding additional oil if necessary. Remove from the heat.

In a large bowl, beat eggs, salt and pepper. Add cheese, bacon and mushrooms; mix well. Stir in potato mixture. Pour into four greased individual baking dishes. Bake, uncovered, at 350° for 25-35 minutes or until a knife inserted near the center comes out clean. Let stand for 5 minutes before serving. **Yield:** 4 servings.

Bacon Hash Brown Bake

I enjoy preparing the hearty breakfasts I serve to my bed-and-breakfast guests. My menu consists of coffee, tea and juice, fresh fruit and a satisfying entree. This tasty side dish has wonderful from-scratch flavor since it starts with fresh potatoes.
—Mark Clark, Twin Mountain, New Hampshire

  4 cups grated cooked potatoes
 12 bacon strips, cooked and crumbled
1/2 cup milk
1/3 cup chopped onion
1/2 teaspoon salt
1/4 teaspoon pepper
1/4 teaspoon garlic powder
  1 tablespoon butter, melted
1/2 teaspoon paprika

In a bowl, combine the first seven ingredients. Transfer to a greased 9-in. pie plate. Drizzle with butter; sprinkle with paprika. Bake at 350° for 35-45 minutes or until lightly browned. **Yield:** 6-8 servings.

Black Hills Golden Egg Bake

(Pictured above right)

I developed this recipe when I was cooking for large groups of people. It's easy to make and gives you plenty of time to do other things while it's baking.
—Sandra Giardino, Rapid City, South Dakota

1/2 cup sliced fresh mushrooms
1/2 cup chopped green pepper
1/4 cup butter
 10 eggs
1/2 cup all-purpose flour
  1 teaspoon baking powder
1/4 teaspoon salt, optional

  1 carton (16 ounces) small-curd cottage cheese
  2 cups (8 ounces) shredded cheddar cheese
  2 cups (8 ounces) shredded Monterey Jack cheese
1/2 pound bulk pork sausage, cooked and drained
  6 bacon strips, cooked and crumbled
  1 can (2-1/4 ounces) sliced ripe olives, drained

In a skillet, saute mushrooms and green pepper in butter until tender. In a mixing bowl, combine eggs, flour, baking powder and salt if desired; mix well. Add mushroom mixture. Stir in remaining ingredients; mix well.

Pour into a greased 13-in. x 9-in. x 2-in. baking dish. Bake, uncovered, at 400° for 15 minutes. Reduce heat to 350°; bake 25-35 minutes longer or until a knife inserted near the center comes out clean. **Yield:** 10-12 servings.

Egg IQ

Refrigerate eggs as soon as you get them home. Keep them in their carton to prevent them from losing moisture and absorbing odors. Fresh eggs are highest in flavor and quality if used within 1 week.

Apple Pan Goody

(Pictured above)

We enjoy this tasty breakfast almost weekly. It's a recipe I found years ago and adapted to my family's taste. The servings are generous and satisfy everyone, even voracious teenagers.
—*Jeanne Bredemeyer, Orient, New York*

    4 to 5 medium tart apples, peeled and
      sliced
  3/4 cup dried cranberries
    6 tablespoons brown sugar
    1 teaspoon ground cinnamon, *divided*
    3 tablespoons butter
    6 eggs
1-1/2 cups orange juice
1-1/2 cups all-purpose flour
  3/4 teaspoon salt
    2 tablespoons sugar
Maple syrup, optional

In a large skillet, saute apples, cranberries, brown sugar and 3/4 teaspoon cinnamon in butter until apples begin to soften, about 6 minutes. Transfer to a greased 13-in. x 9-in. x 2-in. baking dish.

In a blender, combine the eggs, orange juice, flour and salt; cover and process until smooth. Pour over apple mixture. Sprinkle with sugar and remaining cinnamon. Bake, uncovered, at 425° for 20-25 minutes or until a knife inserted near the center

comes out clean. Serve with syrup if desired. **Yield:** 8 servings.

Crab Quiche Bake

(Pictured below)

On a farm, a hearty breakfast is a given. Loaded with cheese, this satisfying crab casserole is an easy-to-assemble addition to a brunch buffet.
—*Nancy Robaidek, Krakow, Wisconsin*

    8 eggs, beaten
    2 cups half-and-half cream
    1 large sweet red pepper, chopped
    1 package (8 ounces) imitation crabmeat,
      chopped
    1 cup soft bread crumbs
    1 cup (4 ounces) shredded Swiss cheese
    1 cup (4 ounces) shredded cheddar
      cheese
  1/2 cup chopped green onions
    1 teaspoon salt
  1/2 teaspoon pepper

In a bowl, combine all of the ingredients. Transfer to a greased 13-in. x 9-in. x 2-in. baking dish. Bake, uncovered, at 350° for 30-35 minutes or until a knife inserted near the center comes out clean. Let stand for 10 minutes before cutting. **Yield:** 6-8 servings.

Amish Breakfast Casserole

We enjoyed a hearty breakfast bake during a visit to an Amish inn. When I asked for the recipe, one of the ladies told me the ingredients right off the top of her head. I modified it to create this version my family loves. Try breakfast sausage in place of the bacon. —Beth Notaro, Kokomo, Indiana

　1 pound sliced bacon, diced
　1 medium sweet onion, chopped
　6 eggs, lightly beaten
　4 cups frozen shredded hash brown
　　potatoes, thawed
　2 cups (8 ounces) shredded cheddar
　　cheese
1-1/2 cups (12 ounces) small-curd cottage
　　cheese
1-1/4 cups shredded Swiss cheese

In a large skillet, cook bacon and onion until bacon is crisp; drain. In a bowl, combine the remaining ingredients; stir in bacon mixture.

Transfer to a greased 13-in. x 9-in. x 2-in. baking dish. Bake, uncovered, at 350° for 35-40 minutes or until set and bubbly. Let stand for 10 minutes before cutting. **Yield:** 12 servings.

Southwest Sausage Bake

(Pictured above)

This layered tortilla dish is not only delicious, but it's a real time-saver because it's put together the night before. The tomato slices provide a nice touch of color. —Barbara Waddel, Lincoln, Nebraska

　6 flour tortillas (10 inches), cut
　　into 1/2-inch strips
　4 cans (4 ounces *each*) chopped green
　　chilies, drained
　1 pound bulk pork sausage, cooked and
　　drained
　2 cups (8 ounces) shredded Monterey
　　Jack cheese
　10 eggs
　1/2 cup milk
　1/2 teaspoon *each* salt, garlic salt, onion
　　salt, pepper and ground cumin
Paprika
　2 medium tomatoes, sliced
Sour cream and salsa

In a greased 13-in. x 9-in. x 2-in. baking dish, layer half of the tortilla strips, chilies, sausage and cheese. Repeat layers. In a bowl, beat the eggs, milk and seasonings; pour over cheese. Sprinkle with paprika. Cover and refrigerate overnight.

Remove from the refrigerator 30 minutes before baking. Bake, uncovered, at 350° for 50 minutes. Arrange tomato slices over the top. Bake 10-15 minutes longer or until a knife inserted near the center comes out clean. Let stand for 10 minutes before cutting. Serve with sour cream and salsa. **Yield:** 12 servings.

Sausage Egg Bake

(Pictured on page 4)

This hearty egg dish is wonderful for any meal of the day, but especially for breakfast. I fix it frequently for special occasions, too, because it's easy to prepare and is really versatile. For a change, use spicier sausage or substitute a flavored cheese blend. —Molly Swallow, Blackfoot, Idaho

　1 pound bulk Italian sausage
　2 cans (10-3/4 ounces *each*) condensed
　　cream of potato soup, undiluted
　9 eggs
　3/4 cup milk
　1/4 teaspoon pepper
　1 cup (4 ounces) shredded cheddar
　　cheese

In a skillet, cook sausage over medium heat until no longer pink; drain. Stir in soup. In a mixing bowl, beat eggs, milk and pepper; stir in sausage mixture.

Transfer to a lightly greased 11-in. x 7-in. x 2-in. baking dish. Sprinkle with cheese. Bake, uncovered, at 375° for 40-45 minutes or until a knife inserted near the center comes out clean. **Yield:** 12 servings.

Hash Brown Casserole

(Pictured below)

I first served this yummy casserole years ago at a family brunch for my husband's birthday. It was such a hit that it became a mainstay at our family get-togethers. It makes a delicious supper, too, served with fruit salad and crusty bread.

—Jan Huntington, Painesville, Ohio

12 eggs
1 can (12 ounces) evaporated milk
1 teaspoon salt
1/2 teaspoon pepper
1/8 teaspoon cayenne pepper, optional
1 package (30 ounces) frozen shredded hash brown potatoes, thawed
2 cups (8 ounces) shredded cheddar cheese
1 large onion, chopped
1 medium green pepper, chopped
1 cup cubed fully cooked ham

In a large bowl, combine the eggs, milk, salt, pepper and cayenne if desired. Stir in the potatoes, cheese, onion, green pepper and ham.

Pour into a greased 13-in. x 9-in. x 2-in. baking dish. Bake, uncovered, at 350° for 45-50 minutes or until a knife inserted near the center comes out clean. **Yield:** 12-15 servings.

Breakfast Bake

This light fluffy egg casserole, sprinkled with tasty bacon, retains its fresh flavor after freezing. While it's great for breakfast, it's an easy-to-reheat meal for lunch or dinner, too. The recipe makes two casseroles, so you can serve one right away and freeze the second one for later.

—Kim Weaver
Olathe, Kansas

4-1/2 cups seasoned croutons
2 cups (8 ounces) shredded cheddar cheese
1 medium onion, chopped
1/4 cup chopped sweet red pepper
1/4 cup chopped green pepper
1 jar (4-1/2 ounces) sliced mushrooms, drained
8 eggs
4 cups milk
1 teaspoon salt
1 teaspoon ground mustard
1/8 teaspoon pepper
8 bacon strips, cooked and crumbled

Sprinkle croutons, cheese, onion, peppers and mushrooms into two greased 8-in. square baking dishes. In a bowl, combine the eggs, milk, salt, mustard and pepper. Slowly pour over vegetables. Sprinkle with bacon.

Cover and freeze one casserole for up to 3 months. Bake the second casserole, uncovered, at 350° for 45-50 minutes or until a knife inserted near the center comes out clean.

To use frozen casserole: Completely thaw in the refrigerator for 24-36 hours. Remove from the refrigerator 30 minutes before baking. Bake, uncovered, at 350° for 50-60 minutes or until a knife inserted near the center comes out clean. **Yield:** 2 casseroles (6-8 servings each).

French Toast Casserole

Cinnamon and sugar top this fuss-free fare that tastes like French toast. Since you assemble it the previous night, you save time in the morning.

—Sharyn Adams, Crawfordsville, Indiana

 Uses less fat, sugar or salt. Includes Nutritional Analysis and Diabetic Exchanges.

1 loaf (10 ounces) French bread, cut into 1-inch cubes (10 cups)
8 eggs
3 cups milk
4 teaspoons sugar
1 teaspoon vanilla extract
3/4 teaspoon salt, optional

TOPPING:
- 2 tablespoons butter, cubed
- 3 tablespoons sugar
- 2 teaspoons ground cinnamon

Maple syrup, optional

Place the bread cubes in a greased 13-in. x 9-in. x 2-in. baking dish. In a mixing bowl, beat the eggs, milk, sugar, vanilla and salt if desired. Pour over the bread. Cover and refrigerate for 8 hours or overnight.

Remove from the refrigerator 30 minutes before baking. Dot with butter. Combine sugar and cinnamon; sprinkle over the top. Cover and bake at 350° for 45-50 minutes or until a knife inserted near the center comes out clean. Let stand for 5 minutes before serving. Serve with syrup if desired. **Yield:** 12 servings.

Nutritional Analysis: One serving (prepared with egg substitute equivalent to 8 eggs, fat-free milk and reduced-fat margarine and without salt and syrup) equals 147 calories, 271 mg sodium, 2 mg cholesterol, 19 g carbohydrate, 9 g protein, 3 g fat, 1 g fiber. **Diabetic Exchanges:** 1 starch, 1 lean meat.

Pineapple Ham Bake

I found this recipe in a church cookbook from my grandfather's hometown. It's simple to fix, and the tangy pineapple flavor goes well with the casserole.
—Patricia Throlson, Hawick, Minnesota

- 2 cans (8 ounces *each*) crushed pineapple, undrained
- 2/3 cup packed brown sugar
- 1 tablespoon vinegar
- 2 teaspoons ground mustard
- 1 pound fully cooked ham, cut into bite-size pieces

Combine the first four ingredients in an ungreased 2-qt. baking dish and mix well. Stir in the ham. Bake, uncovered, at 350° for 30-40 minutes or until heated through. Serve with a slotted spoon. **Yield:** 8 servings.

Sausage Brunch Casserole

(Pictured above right)

I've served this hearty dish to many guests, and they always ask for the recipe. It can even be assembled the night before and kept in the refrigerator. Just pop it in the oven in the morning.
—Paula Christensen, Soldotna, Alaska

- 1 pound bulk pork sausage, cooked and drained
- 1/2 cup chopped green onions
- 1 can (4 ounces) mushroom stems and pieces, drained
- 2 medium tomatoes, chopped
- 2 cups (8 ounces) shredded mozzarella cheese
- 1 cup pancake mix
- 12 eggs
- 1 cup milk
- 1/2 teaspoon dried oregano
- 1/2 teaspoon salt
- 1/4 teaspoon pepper

In a greased 3-qt. baking dish, layer the sausage, onions, mushrooms, tomatoes and cheese. In a large bowl, whisk the pancake mix, eggs, milk, oregano, salt and pepper; pour over cheese.

Bake, uncovered, at 350° for 45-50 minutes or until top is set and lightly browned. Let stand for 10 minutes before serving. **Yield:** 6-8 servings.

Bacon Basics

Pricking bacon with a fork reduces excess curling and helps it lie flat in the pan. Cooked bacon strips can be wrapped and refrigerated for up to 5 days or frozen for up to 6 weeks. They make a quick-and-easy topping for casseroles when thawed and crumbled into small pieces.

Egg and Broccoli Casserole

(Pictured above)

For years, I've prepared this filling egg casserole, which is delicious for brunch, in my slow cooker. It's an unusual recipe for this appliance but is welcomed wherever I serve it. —*Janet Sliter*
Kennewick, Washington

1 carton (24 ounces) small-curd cottage cheese
1 package (10 ounces) frozen chopped broccoli, thawed and drained
2 cups (8 ounces) shredded cheddar cheese
6 eggs, beaten
1/3 cup all-purpose flour
1/4 cup butter, melted
3 tablespoons finely chopped onion
1/2 teaspoon salt
Additional shredded cheddar cheese, optional

In a large bowl, combine the first eight ingredients. Pour into a greased slow cooker. Cover and cook on high for 1 hour. Stir.

Reduce heat to low; cover and cook 2-1/2 to 3 hours longer or until a thermometer placed in the center reads 160° and the eggs are set. Sprinkle with cheese if desired. **Yield:** 6 servings.

BLT Egg Bake

(Pictured at right)

BLTs are a favorite at my house, so I created this recipe to combine those flavors in a "dressier" dish.

It was such a hit, I served it to my church ladies' group at a brunch I hosted. I received lots of compliments and wrote out the recipe many times that day. —*Priscilla Detrick, Catoosa, Oklahoma*

1/4 cup mayonnaise
5 slices bread, toasted
4 slices process American cheese
12 bacon strips, cooked and crumbled
4 eggs
1 medium tomato, halved and sliced
2 tablespoons butter
2 tablespoons all-purpose flour
1/4 teaspoon salt
1/8 teaspoon pepper
1 cup milk
1/2 cup shredded cheddar cheese
2 green onions, thinly sliced
Shredded lettuce

Spread mayonnaise on one side of each slice of toast and cut into small pieces. Arrange toast, mayonnaise side up, in a greased 8-in. square baking dish. Top with cheese slices and bacon. In a skillet, fry eggs over medium heat until completely set; place over bacon. Top with tomato slices; set aside.

In a saucepan, melt butter. Stir in flour, salt and pepper until smooth. Gradually add milk. Bring to a boil; cook and stir for 2 minutes or until thickened. Pour over tomato. Sprinkle with cheddar cheese and onions. Bake, uncovered, at 325° for 10 minutes. Cut into squares; serve with lettuce. **Yield:** 4 servings.

Grits 'n' Sausage Casserole

You could call this the "So Good Casserole" because that's what people say when they try it. It's a Southern specialty. —Marie Poppenhager
Old Town, Florida

        3 cups water
        1 cup quick-cooking grits
    3/4 teaspoon salt, *divided*
        2 pounds bulk pork sausage, cooked and drained
        2 cups (8 ounces) shredded cheddar cheese, *divided*
        3 eggs
    1-1/2 cups milk
        2 tablespoons butter, melted
    Pepper to taste

In a saucepan, bring water to a boil. Slowly whisk in the grits and 1/2 teaspoon salt. Reduce heat; cover and simmer for 5 minutes, stirring occasionally. In a large bowl, combine grits, sausage and 1-1/2 cups cheese. Beat the eggs and milk; stir into grits mixture. Add the butter, pepper and remaining salt.

Transfer to a greased 13-in. x 9-in. x 2-in. baking dish. Bake, uncovered, at 350° for 1 hour or until a knife inserted near the center comes out clean. Sprinkle with remaining cheese; bake 15 minutes longer or until cheese is melted. Let stand for 5 minutes before cutting. **Yield:** 10-12 servings.

Cheese Sausage Strata

Sausage provides plenty of flavor in this hearty morning casserole. It's a great addition to a brunch buffet, because it's assembled the night before to cut down on last-minute fuss. —Teresa Marchese
New Berlin, Wisconsin

    1-1/2 pounds bulk pork sausage
        9 eggs, lightly beaten
        3 cups milk
        9 slices bread, cubed
    1-1/2 cups (6 ounces) shredded cheddar cheese
    1/2 pound sliced bacon, cooked and crumbled
    1-1/2 teaspoons ground mustard

In a large skillet, cook sausage over medium heat until no longer pink; drain. Add eggs, milk, bread, cheese, bacon and mustard. Transfer to a greased shallow 3-qt. baking dish. Cover and chill overnight.

Remove from the refrigerator 30 minutes before baking. Cover and bake at 350° for 60-65 minutes or until a knife inserted near the center comes out clean. **Yield:** 12-15 servings.

Chive-Ham Brunch Bake

(Pictured above)

This casserole is hearty and festive with ham, tomatoes and chives. —Edie DeSpain, Logan, Utah

    1/2 cup chopped onion
        1 tablespoon butter
        1 can (5 ounces) chunk ham, drained
        1 medium tomato, chopped
        2 cups biscuit/baking mix
    1/2 cup water
        1 cup (4 ounces) shredded Swiss *or* cheddar cheese
        2 eggs
    1/4 cup milk
    1/4 teaspoon dill weed
    1/4 teaspoon salt
    1/8 teaspoon pepper
        3 tablespoons minced chives

In a skillet, saute onion in butter until tender. Stir in ham and tomato; set aside. In a bowl, combine biscuit mix and water; mix well. Press onto the bottom and 1/2 in. up the sides of a greased 13-in. x 9-in. x 2-in. baking dish. Spread ham mixture over the crust; sprinkle with cheese.

In a bowl, beat the eggs, milk, dill, salt and pepper; pour over cheese. Sprinkle with chives. Bake, uncovered, at 350° for 25-30 minutes or until a knife inserted near the center comes out clean. **Yield:** 8 servings.

Blueberry Brunch Bake

(Pictured below)

This recipe is especially nice for overnight company. It's simple to make the day before and then pop in the oven in the morning. Just sit back and enjoy your guests and a great breakfast.

—Carol Forcum, Marion, Illinois

    1 loaf (1 pound) day-old French bread, cut into 1/2-inch cubes
1-1/2 cups blueberries
   12 ounces cream cheese, softened
    8 eggs
  1/2 cup plain yogurt
  1/3 cup sour cream
    1 teaspoon vanilla extract
  1/2 teaspoon ground cinnamon
  1/2 cup milk
  1/3 cup maple syrup
Additional blueberries, optional
Additional maple syrup

Place half of the bread cubes in a greased shallow 3-qt. baking dish. Sprinkle with blueberries. In a mixing bowl, beat cream cheese until smooth. Beat in the eggs, yogurt, sour cream, vanilla and cinnamon. Gradually add milk and 1/3 cup syrup until blended. Pour half over the bread. Top with the remaining bread and cream cheese mixture. Cover and refrigerate overnight.

Remove from the refrigerator 30 minutes before baking. Cover and bake at 350° for 30 minutes. Uncover; bake 20-25 minutes longer or until a knife inserted near the center comes out clean. Sprinkle with additional blueberries if desired. Let stand for 5 minutes. Serve with syrup. **Yield:** 6-8 servings.

Breakfast Bread Pudding

This slightly sweet casserole-for-one is a fun alternative to typical breakfast entrees. It's a snap to prepare in the microwave on a busy morning. And it's yummy served warm or cold for dessert, too.

—Anne Morrissey, Marshfield, Massachusetts

✓ Uses less fat, sugar or salt. Includes Nutritional Analysis and Diabetic Exchanges.

    1 slice bread, cut into 1/2-inch cubes
  1/4 cup diced peeled tart apple
    1 tablespoon raisins
  1/2 cup fat-free milk
  1/4 cup egg substitute
  1/2 teaspoon vanilla extract
Sugar substitute equivalent to 2 teaspoons sugar
  1/4 teaspoon apple pie spice

Place bread cubes, apple and raisins in a microwave-safe 2-cup bowl coated with nonstick cooking spray. In another bowl, whisk together the remaining ingredients; pour over bread mixture.

Microwave, uncovered, on high for 3 minutes or until mixture puffs and bubbles around the edges. **Yield:** 1 serving.

Nutritional Analysis: One serving equals 233 calories, 4 g fat (1 g saturated fat), 3 mg cholesterol, 339 mg sodium, 34 g carbohydrate, 2 g fiber, 15 g protein. **Diabetic Exchanges:** 1 starch, 1 lean meat, 1 fruit, 1/2 milk.

Editor's Note: This recipe was tested in an 850-watt microwave.

Green 'n' Gold Egg Bake

I need just five ingredients to assemble this pretty casserole. The firm squares have a delicious spinach flavor that's welcome at breakfast or dinner.

—Muriel Paceleo, Montgomery, New York

    1 cup seasoned bread crumbs, *divided*
    2 packages (10 ounces *each*) frozen chopped spinach, thawed and squeezed dry
    3 cups (24 ounces) small-curd cottage cheese
  1/2 cup grated Romano *or* Parmesan cheese
    5 eggs

Sprinkle 1/4 cup bread crumbs into a greased 8-in. square baking dish. Bake at 350° for 3-5 minutes or until golden brown. In a bowl, combine the spinach, cottage cheese, Romano cheese, three eggs and remaining crumbs. Spread over the baked crumbs. Beat remaining eggs; pour over spinach mixture.

Bake, uncovered, at 350° for 45 minutes or until a knife inserted near the center comes out clean. Let stand for 5-10 minutes before serving. **Yield:** 9 servings.

Chicken Brunch Bake

Chunks of tender chicken add heartiness to this appealing brunch casserole. —DeLee Jochum
Dubuque, Iowa

✓ Uses less fat, sugar or salt. Includes Nutritional Analysis and Diabetic Exchanges.

  9 slices day-old bread, cubed
  3 cups chicken broth
  4 cups cubed cooked chicken
1/2 cup uncooked instant rice
1/2 cup diced pimientos
  2 tablespoons minced fresh parsley
1-1/2 teaspoons salt, optional
  4 eggs, beaten

In a large bowl, toss bread cubes and broth. Add chicken, rice, pimientos, parsley and salt if desired; mix well. Transfer to a greased 13-in. x 9-in. x 2-in. baking dish. Pour eggs over all. Bake, uncovered, at 325° for 1 hour or until a knife inserted near the center comes out clean. **Yield:** 8 servings.
Nutritional Analysis: One serving (prepared with reduced-calorie bread, reduced-sodium broth and egg substitute equivalent to 4 eggs and without salt) equals 179 calories, 242 mg sodium, 44 mg cholesterol, 17 g carbohydrate, 19 g protein, 4 g fat. **Diabetic Exchanges:** 2 lean meat, 1 starch.

Colorful Ham Strata

(Pictured above right)

This make-ahead breakfast bake is a cinch, particularly when leftover ham is used. Chock-full of peppers, onions and cheese, the eye-opener is a great way to start the day. —Marilou Robinson
Portland, Oregon

  2 medium onions, quartered and sliced
3/4 cup *each* julienned green and sweet red pepper
  1 teaspoon olive oil

  1 loaf (1 pound) French bread, cut into 1/2-inch cubes
1-1/2 cups diced fully cooked ham (3/4 pound)
  1 cup (4 ounces) shredded Monterey Jack cheese
  6 eggs
  2 cups milk
  1 teaspoon salt
1/2 teaspoon pepper

In a large skillet, saute onions and peppers in oil. Place half of the bread cubes in a greased 13-in. x 9-in. x 2-in. baking dish. Sprinkle with half of the onion mixture, ham and cheese. Repeat layers. In a bowl, beat the eggs, milk, salt and pepper. Pour over bread mixture. Cover and refrigerate overnight.

Remove from the refrigerator 30 minutes before baking. Bake, uncovered, at 350° for 30-35 minutes or until a knife inserted near the center comes out clean. **Yield:** 6-8 servings.

Too Much Bread?

Wrap and freeze excess bread slices and trimmings (adding to the bag as you have them) and use to make homemade breadcrumbs, stuffing, croutons, bread pudding and more.

Brunch Lasagna

(Pictured below)

A professional cook, I appreciate make-ahead dishes like this one. Pop it into the oven before guests arrive…add fresh fruit and muffins…and you have an instant brunch. You can serve it as a hearty supper, too, drizzled with a little salsa.
—Judy Munger, Warren, Minnesota

    8 uncooked lasagna noodles
    8 eggs
    1/2 cup milk
Butter-flavored nonstick cooking spray
    2 jars (16 ounces *each*) Alfredo sauce
    3 cups diced fully cooked ham
    1/2 cup diced green pepper
    1/4 cup chopped green onions
    1 cup (4 ounces) shredded cheddar
      cheese
    1/4 cup grated Parmesan cheese

Cook noodles according to package directions. Meanwhile, in a large bowl, beat eggs and milk. In a large nonstick skillet coated with butter-flavored cooking spray, cook eggs over medium-low heat until set but moist. Remove from the heat. Drain noodles.

Spread 1/2 cup Alfredo sauce in a greased 10-in. square or 13-in. x 9-in. x 2-in. baking dish. Layer with four lasagna noodles (trim noodles if necessary to fit dish), ham, green pepper and onions.

Toffee Apple French Toast

(Pictured above)

I love quick breakfast recipes that can be assembled the night before, saving time on busy mornings. I created this dish by incorporating my family's favorite apple dip with French toast.
—Reneé Endress, Galva, Illinois

    8 cups cubed French bread (1-inch cubes)
    2 medium tart apples, peeled and
      chopped
    1 package (8 ounces) cream cheese,
      softened
    3/4 cup packed brown sugar
    1/4 cup sugar
  1-3/4 cups milk, *divided*
    2 teaspoons vanilla extract, *divided*
    1/2 cup English toffee bits *or* almond
      brickle chips
    5 eggs

Place half of the bread cubes in a greased 13-in. x 9-in. x 2-in. baking dish; top with apples. In a mixing bowl, beat the cream cheese, sugars, 1/4 cup milk and 1 teaspoon vanilla until smooth; stir in toffee bits. Spread over apples. Top with remaining bread cubes. In another mixing bowl, beat the eggs and remaining milk and vanilla; pour over bread. Cover and refrigerate overnight.

Remove from the refrigerator 30 minutes before baking. Bake, uncovered, at 350° for 35-45 minutes or until a knife inserted near the center comes out clean. **Yield:** 8 servings.

Top with half of the remaining Alfredo sauce and the remaining noodles. Layer with scrambled eggs, cheddar cheese and remaining Alfredo sauce. Sprinkle with Parmesan cheese.

Bake, uncovered, at 375° for 45-50 minutes or until heated through and bubbly. Let stand for 10 minutes before cutting. **Yield:** 10-12 servings.

Spinach-Sausage Egg Bake

(Pictured at right)

I always cook up a storm during the holidays. Spinach and red peppers give festive Christmas color to this satisfying bake that boasts Italian sausage, lots of cheese and a short prep time.
—*Barbara Nowakowski*
North Tonawanda, New York

    1 pound bulk Italian sausage
1/2 cup chopped onion
    1 jar (7 ounces) roasted red peppers,
       drained and chopped, *divided*
    1 package (10 ounces) frozen chopped
       spinach, thawed and squeezed dry
    1 cup all-purpose flour
1/4 cup grated Parmesan cheese
    1 teaspoon dried basil
1/2 teaspoon salt
    8 eggs
    2 cups milk
    1 cup (4 ounces) shredded provolone
       cheese

In a large skillet, cook the sausage and onion over medium heat until the meat is no longer pink; drain. Transfer to a greased 3-qt. baking dish. Sprinkle with half of the red peppers; top with the spinach.

In a bowl, combine the flour, Parmesan cheese, basil and salt. Whisk eggs and milk; stir into flour mixture until blended. Pour over spinach.

Bake, uncovered, at 425° for 15-20 minutes or until a knife inserted near the center comes out clean. Top with provolone cheese and remaining red peppers. Bake 3-5 minutes longer or until cheese is melted. Let stand for 5 minutes before serving. **Yield:** 6 servings.

Artichoke Egg Casserole

This casserole is a great recipe for a brunch. I serve it with fresh stir-fried asparagus, a fruit salad and croissants on the side. —*Marilyn Moores*
Indianapolis, Indiana

    4 jars (6-1/2 ounces *each*) marinated
       artichoke hearts
1/2 cup chopped green onions
    2 to 3 garlic cloves, minced
    1 tablespoon vegetable oil
    8 eggs
    1 jar (4-1/2 ounces) sliced mushrooms,
       drained
    3 cups (12 ounces) shredded sharp
       cheddar cheese
    1 cup butter-flavored cracker crumbs
       (about 25 crackers)

Drain artichokes, reserving 1/2 cup marinade. Set aside. Cut artichokes into slices and set aside. In a skillet, saute green onions and garlic in oil until tender. Remove from the heat.

In a large bowl, beat eggs well. Stir in the artichokes, mushrooms, cheese, cracker crumbs, onion mixture and the reserved marinade.

Transfer to a greased 13-in. x 9-in. x 2-in. baking dish. Bake, uncovered, at 350° for 35-40 minutes or until a knife inserted near the center comes out clean. **Yield:** 9 servings.

Beef

Biscuit Pizza Bake, p. 24

Chapter 2

Beef and Spirals

(Pictured below)

My mom shared this easy-to-assemble casserole years ago. It's very good with garlic toast. Large shell macaroni or ziti noodles can be used instead of spiral pasta.
—*Brenda Marschall*
Poplar Bluff, Missouri

> 2 cups uncooked spiral pasta
> 2 pounds ground beef
> 2 small onions, chopped
> 1 garlic clove, minced
> 1 jar (26 ounces) spaghetti sauce
> 1 jar (4-1/2 ounces) sliced mushrooms, drained
> 1/2 cup sour cream
> 1/2 pound process American cheese, cubed
> 2 cups (8 ounces) shredded mozzarella cheese

Cook pasta according to package directions. Meanwhile, in a large saucepan, cook the beef, onions and garlic over medium heat until meat is no longer pink; drain. Stir in spaghetti sauce and mushrooms; bring to a boil. Reduce heat; cover and simmer for 20 minutes.

Place 1/2 cup of meat sauce in a greased shallow 2-1/2-qt. baking dish. Drain pasta; place half over sauce. Top with half of the remaining meat sauce; spread with sour cream. Top with American cheese and remaining pasta and meat sauce.

Sprinkle with mozzarella cheese. Cover and bake at 350° for 25-30 minutes. Uncover; bake 5-10 minutes longer or until bubbly. **Yield:** 8-10 servings.

Unstuffed Cabbage

I received the recipe for this hearty ground beef and cabbage casserole from a teacher at the preschool where I work. It's a nutritious meal. —*Judy Thorn*
Mars, Pennsylvania

 Uses less fat, sugar or salt. Includes Nutritional Analysis and Diabetic Exchanges.

> 6 cups chopped cabbage
> 1/2 pound ground beef
> 1 small onion, chopped
> 1 cup uncooked instant rice
> 1/2 teaspoon salt, optional
> 1/4 teaspoon pepper
> 2 cans (10-3/4 ounces *each*) condensed tomato soup, undiluted
> 1 cup water
> 1/3 cup shredded cheddar cheese

Place the cabbage in a greased 2-1/2-qt. baking dish. In a skillet, cook beef and onion over medium heat until meat is no longer pink; drain. Stir in the rice, salt if desired and pepper; spoon over cabbage. Combine soup and water; pour over beef mixture.

Cover and bake at 350° for 40-50 minutes or until rice and cabbage are tender. Uncover; sprinkle with cheese. Bake 5-10 minutes longer or until the cheese is melted. **Yield:** 4 servings.

Nutritional Analysis: One serving (prepared with lean ground beef, reduced-fat reduced-sodium tomato soup and reduced-fat cheese and without salt) equals 342 calories, 8 g fat (3 g saturated fat), 23 mg cholesterol, 690 mg sodium, 48 g carbohydrate, 5 g fiber, 19 g protein. **Diabetic Exchanges:** 2-1/2 starch, 2 lean meat, 2 vegetable.

Potato Sloppy Joe Bake

I created this speedy sensation while racing against the clock one day. I needed a quick meal that was low on ingredients but high on taste, so I came up with this hearty casserole. —*Ruth Chiarenza*
Cumberland, Maryland

> 1 pound ground beef
> 1 can (15-1/2 ounces) sloppy joe sauce
> 1 can (10-3/4 ounces) condensed cream of potato soup, undiluted

1 package (32 ounces) frozen cubed hash
  brown potatoes, thawed
1 cup (4 ounces) shredded cheddar
  cheese

In a skillet, cook beef over medium heat until no longer pink; drain. Add sloppy joe sauce and soup. Place hash browns in a greased 13-in. x 9-in. x 2-in. baking dish. Top with beef mixture.

   Cover and bake at 450° for 20 minutes. Uncover; bake 10 minutes longer or until heated through. Sprinkle with cheese. **Yield:** 6-8 servings.

Cheesy Beef Casserole

This hearty casserole tastes like lasagna and makes a satisfying meal when served with a green salad and crusty garlic bread.   —Ardyce Piehl
Wisconsin Dells, Wisconsin

  4 cups uncooked medium egg noodles
  1 pound ground beef
3/4 cup chopped onion
  2 cans (8 ounces *each*) tomato sauce
1/2 teaspoon garlic powder
1/2 teaspoon salt
1/4 teaspoon pepper
  1 package (8 ounces) cream cheese,
    softened
  1 cup (8 ounces) small-curd cottage
    cheese
1/2 cup grated Parmesan cheese
1/3 cup sliced green onions
1/4 cup chopped green pepper
Additional Parmesan cheese, optional

Cook noodles according to package directions. Meanwhile, in a skillet, cook beef and onion over medium heat until meat is no longer pink; drain. Add tomato sauce, garlic powder, salt and pepper. In a mixing bowl, combine the cream cheese, cottage cheese, Parmesan, onions and green pepper.

   Drain the noodles; place half in a greased 13-in. x 9-in. x 2-in. baking dish. Top with half of the meat and cheese mixtures. Repeat layers. Sprinkle with additional Parmesan if desired. Cover and bake at 350° for 30-35 minutes or until heated through. **Yield:** 6 servings.

Easy Taco Casserole

(Pictured above right)

Your family is sure to enjoy this mildly spicy one-dish meal with Southwestern flair. It's quick and easy to make and fun to serve.   —Flo Burtnett
Gage, Oklahoma

  1 pound ground beef
  1 cup salsa
1/2 cup mayonnaise
  2 teaspoons chili powder
  2 cups crushed tortilla chips
  1 cup (4 ounces) shredded Colby cheese
  1 cup (4 ounces) shredded Monterey Jack
    cheese
  1 medium tomato, chopped
  2 cups shredded lettuce

In a skillet, cook beef over medium heat until no longer pink; drain. Add salsa, mayonnaise and chili powder; mix well. In an ungreased 2-qt. baking dish, layer half of the meat mixture, chips and cheeses. Repeat layers.

   Bake, uncovered, at 350° for 20-25 minutes or until heated through. Just before serving, top with tomato and lettuce. **Yield:** 6 servings.

Say Cheese!

To save time, buy packages of cheese that are already sliced or shredded. If you'd rather save money, buy blocks of cheese and slice or shred your own. Most cheeses can be grated ahead of time and refrigerated in a plastic bag until ready to use. If it sticks together, simply break up the pieces with your fingers.

stir until the cheese is melted.

Transfer to a greased 11-in. x 7-in. x 2-in. baking dish. Sprinkle with remaining cheese. Toss bread crumbs with butter; sprinkle over cheese. Bake, uncovered, at 350° for 15-20 minutes or until cheese is melted. **Yield:** 4-6 servings.

Pizza Tot Casserole

(Pictured below)

Since I cook for two, I often divide this upside-down pizza casserole into two smaller casserole dishes—one for dinner and one to freeze. I take the frozen portion out of the freezer the night before to thaw in the fridge before baking.
—*Chris Stukel, Des Plaines, Illinois*

 1 pound ground beef
 1 medium green pepper, chopped
 1 medium onion, chopped
 1 can (10-3/4 ounces) condensed Italian
   tomato with roasted garlic and herb
   soup, undiluted
 1 jar (4-1/2 ounces) sliced mushrooms,
   drained
 2 cups (8 ounces) shredded mozzarella
   cheese
 1 package (32 ounces) frozen Tater Tots

In a skillet, cook the beef, pepper and onion until meat is no longer pink; drain. Add soup and mushrooms. Transfer to a greased 13-in. x 9-in. x 2-in.

Grandma's Rice Dish

(Pictured above)

My grandmother often made this casserole when I was young. I forgot about it until I found myself adding the same ingredients to leftover rice one day. The memories came flooding back, and I've made this recipe regularly since then.
—*Lorna Moore, Glendora, California*

 1 pound ground beef
 1 small onion, chopped
 1/2 cup chopped green pepper
 2 cups cooked long grain rice
 1 can (14-1/2 ounces) diced tomatoes,
   undrained
 1 can (11 ounces) whole kernel corn,
   drained
 1 can (2-1/4 ounces) sliced ripe olives,
   drained
 6 bacon strips, cooked and crumbled
 2 teaspoons chili powder
 1 teaspoon garlic powder
 1 teaspoon salt
1-1/2 cups (6 ounces) shredded cheddar
   cheese, *divided*
 1/2 cup dry bread crumbs
 1 tablespoon butter, melted

In a skillet, cook beef, onion and green pepper over medium heat until meat is no longer pink; drain. Stir in the rice, tomatoes, corn, olives, bacon, chili powder, garlic powder and salt. Bring to a boil; remove from the heat. Add 1 cup of cheese and

baking dish. Top with cheese and potatoes. Bake, uncovered, at 400° for 30-35 minutes or until golden brown. **Yield:** 6-8 servings.

Beef Stuffing Bake

I work full time, so I'm always looking for quick dishes that taste good. This one includes two of my kids' favorite foods—ground beef and stuffing.
—Denise Goedeken, Platte Center, Nebraska

1 pound ground beef
1 small onion, chopped
1 package (10 ounces) beef- *or* pork-
  flavored stuffing mix
1 can (10-3/4 ounces) condensed cream of
  celery soup, undiluted
1 can (10-3/4 ounces) condensed cream of
  mushroom soup, undiluted
1 jar (4-1/2 ounces) sliced mushrooms,
  drained
1 cup water
1 cup frozen mixed vegetables

In a skillet, cook beef and onion over medium heat until meat is no longer pink; drain. Transfer to an ungreased 13-in. x 9-in. x 2-in. baking dish.
  In a bowl, combine contents of stuffing seasoning packet, soups, mushrooms, water and vegetables. Sprinkle stuffing over beef mixture; top with soup mixture. Bake, uncovered, at 350° for 30 minutes or until heated through. **Yield:** 6-8 servings.

Tasty Hamburger Casserole

I need just a few ingredients to pack a lot of flavor into this hearty ground beef bake. My daughter received this recipe from a missionary when she was serving in Zambia. It's delicious.
—Faith Richards, Tampa, Florida

5 medium potatoes, peeled and sliced
1 small onion, chopped
1 pound ground beef
1 can (10-3/4 ounces) condensed cream of
  mushroom soup, undiluted
1 can (10-1/2 ounces) condensed
  vegetarian vegetable soup, undiluted
1 cup crushed potato chips

In a greased 13-in. x 9-in. x 2-in. baking dish, layer the potatoes and onion. Crumble beef over onion. Spread soups over beef. Cover and bake at 350° for 55 minutes. Uncover; sprinkle with chips. Bake 20 minutes longer or until meat is no longer pink. **Yield:** 4-6 servings.

Cajun Cabbage

(Pictured above)

Looking for a different treatment for cabbage? Try this spicy cheese-topped dish that I adapted from a friend's recipe. Not only do my husband and kids like it, I get rave reviews when I make it for company or church functions. —Bobbie Soileau
Opelousas, Louisiana

1 pound ground beef
1 medium green pepper, chopped
1 medium onion, chopped
2 garlic cloves, minced
1 can (10 ounces) diced tomatoes and
  green chilies
1 can (8 ounces) tomato sauce
1/2 cup uncooked long grain rice
1 teaspoon salt
1/2 teaspoon dried basil
1/2 teaspoon dried oregano
1/4 to 1/2 teaspoon *each* white, black and
  cayenne pepper
4 to 6 drops hot pepper sauce
1 small head cabbage, chopped
1 cup (4 ounces) shredded Colby cheese

In a skillet, cook beef, green pepper, onion and garlic over medium heat until meat is no longer pink; drain. Stir in tomatoes, tomato sauce, rice and seasonings. Spread into an ungreased 13-in. x 9-in. x 2-in. baking dish. Top with cabbage and cheese. Cover; bake at 350° for 65-75 minutes or until the rice is tender. **Yield:** 6-8 servings.

Sloppy Joe Under a Bun

(Pictured below)

I usually keep a can of sloppy joe sauce in the pantry because our kids love sloppy joes. But sometimes I don't have buns on hand. With this fun casserole, we can still enjoy the flavor that they love in a flash. The bun-like top crust is made with biscuit mix, sprinkled with sesame seeds and baked until golden. —Trish Bloom, Romeo, Michigan

1-1/2 pounds ground beef
  1 can (15-1/2 ounces) sloppy joe sauce
  2 cups (8 ounces) shredded cheddar
    cheese
  2 cups biscuit/baking mix
  2 eggs, beaten
  1 cup milk
  1 tablespoon sesame seeds

In a skillet, cook beef over medium heat until no longer pink; drain. Stir in sloppy joe sauce; mix well. Transfer to a lightly greased 13-in. x 9-in. x 2-in. baking dish; sprinkle with cheese.

In a bowl, combine biscuit mix, eggs and milk just until blended. Pour over cheese; sprinkle with sesame seeds. Bake, uncovered, at 400° for 25 minutes or until golden brown. **Yield:** 8 servings.

Biscuit Pizza Bake

(Pictured on page 18 and front cover)

This recipe provides all the flavor of traditional pizza in a convenient casserole. It's chock-full of ground beef, pepperoni and veggies.
—Emma Hageman, Waucoma, Iowa

  1 pound ground beef
  2 tubes (12 ounces *each*) refrigerated
    buttermilk biscuits
  1 can (15 ounces) pizza sauce
  1 cup chopped green pepper
1/2 cup chopped onion
  1 can (4 ounces) mushroom stems and
    pieces, drained
  1 package (3-1/2 ounces) sliced pepperoni
  1 cup (4 ounces) shredded mozzarella
    cheese
  1 cup (4 ounces) shredded cheddar
    cheese

In a skillet, cook beef over medium heat until no longer pink. Meanwhile, quarter the biscuits; place in a greased shallow 3-qt. baking dish. Top with pizza sauce. Drain beef; sprinkle over biscuits and sauce. Layer with green pepper, onion, mushrooms, pepperoni and cheeses.

Bake, uncovered, at 350° for 25-30 minutes or until cheese is melted. Let stand for 5-10 minutes before serving. **Yield:** 6-8 servings.

Lasagna Casserole

This hearty main dish retains the wonderful taste of the traditional favorite without all the work. I recently tried sausage rather than ground beef, and everyone raved about the added spiciness.
—Deb Morrison, Skiatook, Oklahoma

  1 pound ground beef
1/4 cup chopped onion
1/2 teaspoon salt
1/2 teaspoon pepper, *divided*
  1 pound medium shell pasta, cooked and
    drained
  1 pound (4 cups) shredded mozzarella
    cheese, *divided*
  3 cups (24 ounces) small-curd cottage
    cheese
  2 eggs, beaten
1/3 cup grated Parmesan cheese

**2 tablespoons dried parsley flakes
1 jar (26 ounces) spaghetti sauce**

In a skillet, cook beef and onion over medium heat until meat is no longer pink and onion is tender; drain. Sprinkle with salt and 1/4 teaspoon pepper; set aside.

In a large bowl, combine pasta, 3 cups of mozzarella cheese, cottage cheese, eggs, Parmesan cheese, parsley and remaining pepper; stir gently. Pour into a greased 13-in. x 9-in. x 2-in. or shallow 3-qt. baking dish. Top with the beef mixture and spaghetti sauce (dish will be full).

Cover and bake at 350° for 45 minutes. Sprinkle with remaining mozzarella. Bake, uncovered, 15 minutes longer or until the cheese is melted and bubbly. Let stand 10 minutes before serving. **Yield: 6-8 servings.**

Mexican Chip Casserole

This satisfying casserole relies on convenient packaged ingredients to create an entree with savory Southwestern flair. There's nothing tricky about the preparation.
                                    —*Doris Heath*
                          Franklin, North Carolina

**1 pound ground beef
1 medium onion, chopped
1 garlic clove, minced
1 can (10-3/4 ounces) condensed cream of mushroom soup, undiluted
1 can (11 ounces) Mexicorn
1 can (4 ounces) chopped green chilies
1 package (10-1/2 ounces) corn chips
1 can (10 ounces) enchilada sauce
1 to 2 cups (4 to 8 ounces) shredded Colby-Monterey Jack cheese**

In a skillet, cook beef, onion and garlic over medium heat until meat is no longer pink and onion is tender; drain. Add soup, corn and chilies; mix well.

In an ungreased shallow 3-qt. baking dish, layer meat mixture, corn chips and enchilada sauce; top with cheese. Bake, uncovered, at 350° for 8-10 minutes or until heated through. **Yield: 6 servings.**

Creamy Corned Beef Bake

(Pictured above right)

I remember my grandmother making this comforting casserole when my family visited her. Now that I'm married, I fix it for my husband and me as an easy evening meal that provides great leftovers for lunch. —*Brenda Myers, Overland Park, Kansas*

**1-1/2 cups cubed cooked corned beef *or* 1 can (12 ounces) cooked corned beef
1 can (10-3/4 ounces) condensed cream of chicken soup, undiluted
8 ounces cheddar cheese, cubed
1 package (7 ounces) small shell pasta, cooked and drained
1 cup milk
1/2 cup chopped onion
2 bread slices, cubed
2 tablespoons butter, melted**

In a bowl, combine first six ingredients. Transfer to a greased 2-qt. baking dish. Toss bread cubes with butter; sprinkle over top. Bake, uncovered, at 350° for 40-45 minutes or until golden brown. Let stand 10 minutes before serving. **Yield: 4 servings.**

Beef in Brief

For speedy meal preparation, cook several pounds of ground beef over medium heat, with chopped onion and minced garlic if you like, until no longer pink. Drain and cool. Then freeze in heavy-duty resealable plastic bags or freezer containers for up to 3 months. One pound of uncooked ground beef will yield 2-1/2 to 3 cups of cooked.

soup mixture. Transfer to a greased 13-in. x 9-in. x 2-in. baking dish. Arrange meatballs over top, pressing lightly into mixture. Cover and bake at 350° for 45 minutes. Uncover; bake 15 minutes longer or until meat is no longer pink and potatoes are tender. **Yield:** 8 servings.

Chili Spaghetti

(Pictured below)

This recipe is a family favorite. It has all the flavor of a zesty bowl of chili in a hearty, more-filling casserole. We especially enjoy it during the colder winter months. —Pam Thompson, Girard, Illinois

> 1 pound ground beef
> 1/2 cup chopped onion
> 2 garlic cloves, minced
> 3 cups tomato juice
> 1 can (16 ounces) kidney beans, rinsed and drained
> 6 ounces spaghetti, broken into 3-inch pieces
> 1 tablespoon Worcestershire sauce
> 2 to 3 teaspoons chili powder
> 1 teaspoon salt
> 1/2 teaspoon pepper

In a skillet over medium heat, cook beef, onion and garlic until meat is no longer pink; drain. Trans-

Meatball Hash Brown Bake

(Pictured above)

For a potluck at church, I wanted to create a recipe that would incorporate a meat dish and side dish in one. This casserole proved to be a crowd-pleaser, and I was asked by many to share my recipe.
> *—Jo Ann Fritzler, Belen, New Mexico*

> 2 eggs
> 3/4 cup crushed saltines (about 20 crackers)
> 6 to 8 garlic cloves, minced
> 2 teaspoons salt, *divided*
> 1-1/2 teaspoons pepper, *divided*
> 1 pound ground beef
> 1 can (10-3/4 ounces) condensed cream of chicken soup, undiluted
> 1 cup (8 ounces) sour cream
> 1 cup (4 ounces) shredded cheddar cheese
> 1 large onion, chopped
> 1 package (30 ounces) frozen shredded hash brown potatoes, thawed

In a bowl, lightly beat eggs. Stir in cracker crumbs, garlic, 1 teaspoon salt and 1/2 teaspoon pepper. Crumble beef over mixture; mix well. Shape into 1-in. balls. In a covered skillet over low heat, cook the meatballs in a small amount of water until browned; drain.

In a bowl, combine the soup, sour cream, cheese, onion and remaining salt and pepper. With paper towels, pat hash browns dry. Stir into the

fer to a greased 2-1/2-qt. baking dish; stir in the remaining ingredients. Cover and bake at 350° for 65-70 minutes or until spaghetti is just tender. Let stand, covered, for 10 minutes. **Yield:** 6 servings.

Enchilada Casserole

This zippy Mexican casserole is a real winner at our house. It's so flavorful and filling, we usually just accompany it with rice and black beans. If your family has spicier tastes, increase the chili powder and use a medium or hot salsa. —Julie Huffman
New Lebanon, Ohio

1-1/2 pounds ground beef
   1 large onion, chopped
   1 cup water
   2 to 3 tablespoons chili powder
1-1/2 teaspoons salt
  1/2 teaspoon pepper
  1/4 teaspoon garlic powder
   2 cups salsa, *divided*
  10 flour tortillas (7 inches) cut into 3/4-inch
     strips, *divided*
   1 cup (8 ounces) sour cream
   2 cans (15-1/4 ounces *each*) whole kernel
     corn, drained
   4 cups (16 ounces) shredded mozzarella
     cheese

In a skillet, cook beef and onion over medium heat until meat is no longer pink; drain. Stir in water, chili powder, salt, pepper and garlic powder. Bring to a boil. Reduce heat; simmer, uncovered, 10 minutes.

Place 1/4 cup salsa each in two greased 8-in. square baking dishes. Layer each dish with a fourth of the tortillas and 1/4 cup salsa. Divide the meat mixture, sour cream and corn between the two casseroles. Top with remaining tortillas, salsa and cheese.

Cover and freeze one casserole for up to 1 month. Cover and bake second casserole at 350° for 35 minutes. Uncover; bake 5-10 minutes longer or until heated through.

To use frozen casserole: Thaw in the refrigerator for 24 hours. Remove from the refrigerator 30 minutes before baking. Bake as directed above. **Yield:** 2 casseroles (4-6 servings each).

Spinach Beef Biscuit Bake

(Pictured above right)

My family is from Greece, and I grew up on Greek food. I also like comfort foods like casseroles, so I

combined the two in this deliciously different main dish. I've served this to both family and friends, and it's a hit with everyone. —Bonnie Bootz
Scottsdale, Arizona

   2 tubes (7-1/2 ounces *each*) refrigerated
     buttermilk biscuits
1-1/2 pounds ground beef
  1/2 cup finely chopped onion
   2 eggs
   1 package (10 ounces) frozen chopped
     spinach, thawed and squeezed dry
   1 can (4 ounces) mushroom stems and
     pieces, drained
   4 ounces crumbled feta *or* shredded
     Monterey Jack cheese
  1/4 cup grated Parmesan cheese
1-1/2 teaspoons garlic powder
Salt and pepper to taste
   1 to 2 tablespoons butter, melted

Press and flatten the biscuits onto the bottom and up the sides of a greased 11-in. x 7-in. x 2-in. baking dish; set aside. In a skillet over medium heat, cook beef and onion until the meat is no longer pink; drain.

In a bowl, beat eggs. Add spinach and mushrooms; mix well. Stir in the cheeses, garlic powder, salt, pepper and beef mixture; mix well. Spoon into prepared crust. Drizzle with butter. Bake, uncovered, at 375° for 25-30 minutes or until crust is lightly browned. **Yield:** 6 servings.

Corned Beef 'n' Cabbage Casserole

(Pictured below)

The comic strip Maggie and Jiggs inspired me to serve this meal. Whenever Maggie asked Jiggs what he would like her to cook, he answered, "Corned beef and cabbage." My husband liked this meal, too, and I always enjoyed making it for potluck suppers and other gatherings.
— Daisy Lewis
Jasper, Alabama

1 medium head cabbage, shredded
  (about 8 cups)
1 small onion, chopped
1 cup water
1 can (15-1/2 ounces) white hominy,
  rinsed and drained
3/4 pound thinly sliced corned beef,
  chopped
1/4 teaspoon salt
1/4 teaspoon pepper
1/4 teaspoon hot pepper sauce

In a large Dutch oven or saucepan, combine cabbage, onion and water; bring to a boil. Reduce heat; cover and simmer for 15 minutes or until the cabbage is tender. Add remaining ingredients; simmer for 5 minutes. **Yield:** 6 servings.

Beef Veggie Casserole

This satisfying casserole is a breeze to fix because it uses leftover roast beef and refrigerated biscuits. With hearty chunks of potato and plenty of mixed vegetables, it makes a wonderful meal with a loaf of garlic bread.
— Patti Keith
Ebensburg, Pennsylvania

1 envelope mushroom gravy mix
3/4 cup water
2 cups cubed cooked beef
2 cups frozen mixed vegetables, thawed
2 medium potatoes, peeled, cooked and
  cubed
1 tube (12 ounces) refrigerated buttermilk
  biscuits, separated into 10 biscuits

In a saucepan, combine gravy mix and water until smooth. Bring to a boil; cook and stir for 1 minute or until thickened. Stir in beef, mixed vegetables and potatoes; heat through.

Transfer to a greased 8-in. square baking dish. Top with biscuits. Bake at 400° for 12-16 minutes or until biscuits are golden and meat mixture is bubbly. **Yield:** 5 servings.

Greek Pasta and Beef

This delightfully different casserole gives everyday macaroni and cheese an international flavor. A co-worker who's a pro at Greek cooking shared the recipe years ago. It brings raves whenever I serve it.
— Dorothy Bateman
Carver, Massachusetts

1 pound ground beef
1 large onion, chopped
1 garlic clove, minced
1 can (8 ounces) tomato sauce
1/2 cup water
1 teaspoon salt
1/2 teaspoon ground cinnamon
1/4 teaspoon ground nutmeg
1/4 teaspoon pepper
1 pound elbow macaroni, cooked and
  drained
1 egg, lightly beaten
1/2 cup grated Parmesan cheese
SAUCE:
1/4 cup butter
1/4 cup all-purpose flour
1/4 teaspoon ground cinnamon

3 cups milk
2 eggs, lightly beaten
1/3 cup grated Parmesan cheese

In a skillet, cook beef, onion and garlic over medium heat until meat is no longer pink; drain. Stir in tomato sauce, water and seasonings. Cover and simmer for 10 minutes, stirring occasionally. Meanwhile, in a bowl, combine macaroni, egg and Parmesan cheese; set aside.

In a large saucepan, melt the butter; stir in the flour and cinnamon until smooth. Gradually add the milk. Bring to a boil over medium heat; cook and stir for 2 minutes or until slightly thickened. Remove from the heat; cool slightly. Stir a small amount of the hot mixture into eggs; return all to pan. Cook and stir for 2 minutes. Remove from the heat; stir in the cheese.

In a greased 3-qt. baking dish, spread half of the macaroni mixture. Top with the beef mixture and the remaining macaroni mixture. Pour the sauce over the top. Bake, uncovered, at 350° for 45-50 minutes or until mixture is bubbly and heated through. Let stand for 5 minutes before serving. **Yield:** 12 servings.

Chilies Rellenos Casserole

I love to cook with chili peppers and use recipes featuring them when I entertain. This recipe has big pepper flavor in every bite. —Nadine Estes
Alto, New Mexico

    1 can (7 ounces) whole green chilies
1-1/2 cups (6 ounces) shredded
        Colby-Monterey Jack cheese
    3/4 pound ground beef
    1/4 cup chopped onion
      1 cup milk
      4 eggs
    1/4 cup all-purpose flour
    1/4 teaspoon salt
    1/8 teaspoon pepper

Split chilies and remove seeds; dry on paper towels. Arrange chilies on the bottom of a greased 2-qt. baking dish. Top with cheese. In a skillet, cook beef and onion over medium heat until meat is no longer pink; drain. Spoon over the cheese. In a mixing bowl, beat milk, eggs, flour, salt and pepper until smooth; pour over beef mixture.

Bake, uncovered, at 350° for 45-50 minutes or until a knife inserted near the center comes out clean. Let stand 5 minutes before serving. **Yield:** 6 servings.

Editor's Note: When cutting or seeding hot peppers, use rubber or plastic gloves to protect your hands. Avoid touching your face.

Zippy Beef Bake

(Pictured above)

With its south-of-the-border flavor, this filling meal-in-one is a family favorite. In fact, we like it so much we have it about once a week! —Gay Kelley
Tucson, Arizona

    3/4 pound ground beef
      1 tablespoon butter
      2 medium zucchini, thinly sliced
    1/4 pound fresh mushrooms, sliced
      2 tablespoons sliced green onions
1-1/2 teaspoons chili powder
      1 teaspoon salt
    1/8 teaspoon garlic powder
1-1/2 cups cooked rice
      1 can (4 ounces) chopped green chilies
    1/2 cup sour cream
      1 cup (4 ounces) shredded Monterey Jack
        cheese, *divided*

In a large skillet over medium heat, cook beef until no longer pink. Add butter, zucchini, mushrooms and onions; cook and stir until vegetables are tender. Drain. Stir in chili powder, salt and garlic powder. Add rice, chilies, sour cream and half of the cheese.

Transfer to a greased 2-qt. baking dish; top with remaining cheese. Bake, uncovered, at 350° for 20 minutes or until cheese is melted. **Yield:** 4 servings.

Cheeseburger 'n' Fries Casserole

(Pictured above)

There are only four ingredients in this quick recipe, and you're likely to have them all on hand. Kids love it because, as the name suggests, it combines two of their favorite fast foods. —Karen Owen
Rising Sun, Indiana

- 2 pounds ground beef
- 1 can (10-3/4 ounces) condensed golden mushroom soup, undiluted
- 1 can (10-3/4 ounces) condensed cheddar cheese soup, undiluted
- 1 package (20 ounces) frozen crinkle-cut French fries

In a skillet, cook beef over medium heat until no longer pink; drain. Stir in soups. Pour into a greased 13-in. x 9-in. x 2-in. baking dish. Arrange French fries on top. Bake, uncovered, at 350° for 50-55 minutes or until the fries are golden brown. **Yield:** 6-8 servings.

Mashed Potato Beef Casserole

(Pictured at right)

This recipe came out of my mother's cookbook. The tarragon really comes through to make a flavorful main dish. —Helen McGeorge
Abbotsford, British Columbia

- 2 bacon strips, diced
- 1 pound ground beef
- 1 large onion, finely chopped
- 1/4 pound fresh mushrooms, sliced
- 1 large carrot, finely chopped
- 1 celery rib, finely chopped
- 3 tablespoons all-purpose flour
- 1 cup beef broth
- 1 tablespoon Worcestershire sauce
- 1 teaspoon dried tarragon
- 1/4 teaspoon pepper
- 3 cups hot mashed potatoes
- 3/4 cup shredded cheddar cheese, *divided*
Paprika

In a skillet, cook bacon until crisp; drain, reserving 1 teaspoon drippings. Set bacon aside. Cook beef in drippings over medium heat until no longer pink; drain. Toss onion, mushrooms, carrot and celery in flour; add to skillet with the broth, Worcestershire sauce, tarragon and pepper.

Bring to a boil; reduce heat. Simmer, uncovered, for 15-20 minutes or until the vegetables are tender. Add bacon; transfer to a greased 2-qt. baking dish. Combine potatoes and 1/2 cup of cheese; spread over beef mixture. Sprinkle with paprika and remaining cheese.

Bake, uncovered, at 350° for 20-25 minutes or until heated through. Broil 4 in. from the heat for 5 minutes or until bubbly. **Yield:** 4-6 servings.

Firecracker Casserole

I loved this Southwestern casserole when my mother made it years ago. Now my husband enjoys it.
—Teressa Eastman, El Dorado, Kansas

2 pounds ground beef
1 medium onion, chopped
1 can (15 ounces) black beans, rinsed and drained
1 to 2 tablespoons chili powder
2 to 3 teaspoons ground cumin
1/2 teaspoon salt
4 flour tortillas (7 inches)
1 can (10-3/4 ounces) condensed cream of mushroom soup, undiluted
1 can (10 ounces) diced tomatoes and green chilies, undrained
1 cup (4 ounces) shredded cheddar cheese

In a skillet over medium heat, cook the beef and onion until the meat is no longer pink; drain. Add beans, chili powder, cumin and salt. Transfer to a greased 13-in. x 9-in. x 2-in. baking dish. Arrange tortillas over the top.

Combine soup and tomatoes; pour over the tortillas. Sprinkle with cheese. Bake, uncovered, at 350° for 25-30 minutes or until heated through. **Yield:** 8 servings.

Pizza Macaroni Bake

What do you get when you combine macaroni and cheese with pizza fixings? This family-pleasing casserole!
—Nancy Porterfield
Gap Mills, West Virginia

1 package (7-1/4 ounces) macaroni and cheese dinner mix
6 cups water
1 pound ground beef
1 medium onion, chopped
1 small green pepper, chopped
1 cup (4 ounces) shredded cheddar cheese
1 jar (14 ounces) pizza sauce
1 package (3-1/2 ounces) sliced pepperoni
1 cup (4 ounces) shredded mozzarella cheese

Set cheese packet from dinner mix aside. In a saucepan, bring water to a boil. Add macaroni; cook 8-10 minutes or until tender. Meanwhile, in a large skillet, cook beef, onion and green pepper over medium heat until meat is no longer pink; drain.

Drain macaroni; stir in contents of cheese packet. Transfer to a greased 13-in. x 9-in. x 2-in. baking dish. Sprinkle with cheddar cheese. Top with beef mixture, pizza sauce, pepperoni and mozzarella. Bake, uncovered, at 350° for 20-25 minutes or until heated through. **Yield:** 6-8 servings.

Four-Pasta Beef Bake

(Pictured above)

This hearty casserole looks and tastes a lot like lasagna, but it's quicker to prepare.
—Harriet Stichter, Milford, Indiana

8 cups uncooked pasta (four different shapes)
2 pounds ground beef
2 medium green peppers, chopped
2 medium onions, chopped
2 cups sliced fresh mushrooms
4 jars (26 ounces *each*) meatless spaghetti sauce
2 eggs, lightly beaten
4 cups (16 ounces) shredded mozzarella cheese

Cook pasta according to package directions. Meanwhile, in a large skillet, cook the beef, green peppers, onions and mushrooms over medium heat until meat is no longer pink; drain.

Drain pasta and place in a large bowl; stir in the beef mixture, two jars of spaghetti sauce and eggs. Transfer to two greased 13-in. x 9-in. x 2-in. baking dishes. Top with remaining sauce; sprinkle with cheese. Bake, uncovered, at 350° for 25-30 minutes or until heated through. **Yield:** 2 casseroles (8-10 servings each).

Olé Polenta Casserole

(Pictured below)

This casserole has been a family favorite for over 25 years! Servings are great dolloped with sour cream. —Angie Biggin, Lyons, Illinois

> 1 cup yellow cornmeal
> 1 teaspoon salt
> 4 cups water, *divided*
> 1 pound ground beef
> 1 cup chopped onion
> 1/2 cup chopped green pepper
> 2 garlic cloves, minced
> 1 can (14-1/2 ounces) diced tomatoes, undrained
> 1 can (8 ounces) tomato sauce
> 1/2 pound sliced fresh mushrooms
> 1 teaspoon *each* dried basil, oregano and dill weed
> Dash hot pepper sauce
> 1-1/2 cups (6 ounces) shredded mozzarella cheese, *divided*
> 1/4 cup grated Parmesan cheese, *divided*

For polenta, in a small bowl, whisk cornmeal, salt and 1 cup water until smooth. In a large saucepan, bring remaining water to a boil. Add cornmeal mixture, stirring constantly. Bring to a boil; cook and stir for 3 minutes or until thickened.

Reduce heat to low; cover and cook for 15 minutes. Divide mixture between two greased 8-in. square baking dishes. Cover and refrigerate until firm, about 1-1/2 hours.

In a large skillet, cook beef, onion, green pepper and garlic over medium heat until meat is no longer pink; drain. Stir in the tomatoes, tomato sauce, mushrooms, herbs and hot pepper sauce; bring to a boil. Reduce heat; simmer, uncovered, for 20 minutes or until thickened.

Loosen one polenta from sides and bottom of dish; invert onto a waxed paper-lined baking sheet and set aside. Spoon half of the meat mixture over the polenta still in dish. Sprinkle with half of the mozzarella and half the Parmesan cheese. Top with the reserved polenta and remaining meat mixture.

Cover and bake at 350° for 40 minutes or until heated through. Uncover; sprinkle with remaining cheese. Bake 5 minutes longer or until cheese is melted. Let stand for 10 minutes before cutting. **Yield:** 6 servings.

Beef Spinach Hot Dish

My family, which includes my parents and six brothers and sisters, all love this recipe. Sometimes I use ground turkey in place of the ground beef with equally delicious results. —Rachel Jones Roland, Arkansas

> 1 pound ground beef
> 1 medium onion, chopped
> 2 garlic cloves, minced
> 1 can (4 ounces) mushroom stems and pieces, drained
> 1 teaspoon salt
> 1 teaspoon dried oregano
> 1/4 teaspoon pepper
> 2 packages (10 ounces *each*) frozen chopped spinach, thawed and squeezed dry
> 1 can (10-3/4 ounces) condensed cream of celery soup, undiluted
> 1 cup (8 ounces) sour cream
> 2 cups (8 ounces) shredded mozzarella cheese, *divided*

In a large skillet, cook beef, onion and garlic over medium heat until the meat is no longer pink; drain. Stir in the mushrooms, salt, oregano and pepper. Add the spinach, soup and sour cream. Stir in half of the mozzarella cheese.

Transfer to a greased 2-qt. baking dish. Bake, uncovered, at 350° for 15 minutes. Sprinkle with the remaining cheese; bake 5 minutes longer or until cheese is melted. **Yield:** 6-8 servings.

Beef and Potato Moussaka

(Pictured at right)

My son brought home this recipe for moussaka (a classic Greek entree) when he had a sixth-grade assignment about Greece. It earned high marks when we made it for his class. Everyone loves the hearty meat-and-potatoes combination.
　　　　—Jean Puffer, Chilliwack, British Columbia

  1 pound ground beef
  1 medium onion, chopped
  1 garlic clove, minced
3/4 cup water
  1 can (6 ounces) tomato paste
  3 tablespoons minced fresh parsley
  1 teaspoon salt
1/2 teaspoon dried mint, optional
1/4 teaspoon ground cinnamon
1/4 teaspoon pepper
PARMESAN SAUCE:
1/4 cup butter
1/4 cup all-purpose flour
  2 cups milk
  4 eggs, beaten
1/2 cup grated Parmesan cheese
1/2 teaspoon salt
  5 medium potatoes, peeled and
　　 thinly sliced

In a large skillet, cook the beef, onion and garlic over medium heat until meat is no longer pink; drain. Stir in the water, tomato paste, parsley, salt, mint if desired, cinnamon and pepper. Set aside.

For sauce, melt butter in a saucepan over medium heat. Stir in the flour until smooth; gradually add milk. Bring to a boil; cook and stir for 2 minutes or until thickened. Remove from the heat. Stir a small amount of hot mixture into eggs; return all to the pan, stirring constantly. Add the Parmesan cheese and salt.

Place half of the potato slices in a greased shallow 3-qt. baking dish. Top with half of the Parmesan sauce and all of the meat mixture. Arrange the remaining potatoes over meat mixture; top with the remaining Parmesan sauce.

Bake, uncovered, at 350° for 1 hour or until potatoes are tender. Let stand for 10 minutes before serving. **Yield:** 8-10 servings.

Italian Spaghetti Bake

This hearty casserole recipe makes two large baking dishes. The tasty layers of meat sauce, spaghetti and gooey cheese are sure to appeal to pizza-loving kids...and adults. You'll bring home empty pans when you take this to a potluck.
　　　　—Janice Fredrickson, Elgin, Texas

   2 packages (one 16 ounces,
　　 one 8 ounces) spaghetti
1-1/2 pounds ground beef
   1 large green pepper, chopped
   1 medium onion, chopped
   2 cans (15 ounces *each*) tomato sauce
   1 package (8 ounces) sliced pepperoni
   1 can (8 ounces) mushroom stems and
　　 pieces, drained
   1 can (3.8 ounces) sliced ripe olives,
　　 drained
 1/2 teaspoon dried basil
 1/2 teaspoon dried oregano
 1/4 teaspoon garlic salt
 1/4 teaspoon pepper
   3 cups (12 ounces) shredded
　　 mozzarella cheese
 1/2 cup grated Parmesan cheese

Cook spaghetti according to package directions. Meanwhile, in a large saucepan, cook the beef, green pepper and onion over medium heat until meat is no longer pink; drain. Stir in the tomato sauce, pepperoni, mushrooms, olives and seasonings. Drain spaghetti.

Spoon 1 cup meat sauce into each of two greased 13-in. x 9-in. x 2-in. baking dishes. Top each with about 2-1/2 cups spaghetti, 1-1/2 cups meat sauce, and remaining spaghetti and meat sauce. Sprinkle with cheeses.

Bake, uncovered, at 350° for 20-25 minutes or until heated through. **Yield:** 2 casseroles (8-10 servings each).

Poultry

Chicken Noodle Casserole, p. 40

Chapter 3

Thanksgiving in a Pan

(Pictured below)

This meal-in-one tastes like a big holiday dinner without the work. It's a great way to use up left-over turkey, but I often use thick slices of deli turkey instead. —Lynne Hahn, Temecula, California

        1 package (6 ounces) stuffing mix
    2-1/2 cups cubed cooked turkey
        2 cups frozen cut green beans, thawed
        1 jar (12 ounces) turkey gravy
    Pepper to taste

Prepare stuffing mix according to package directions. Transfer to a greased 11-in. x 7-in. x 2-in. baking dish. Top with turkey, beans, gravy and pepper. Cover and bake at 350° for 30-35 minutes or until heated through. **Yield:** 6 servings.

Avocado Chicken Casserole

Avocados look luscious in this easy layered casserole, and they melt in your mouth.
—Martha Sue Stroud, Clarksville, Texas

    1/4 cup butter
    1/4 cup all-purpose flour
    1/2 teaspoon salt

    1/4 teaspoon *each* garlic powder, onion powder, dried basil, marjoram and thyme
    1-1/2 cups milk
        1 cup half-and-half cream
        8 ounces medium egg noodles, cooked and drained
        3 medium ripe avocados, peeled and sliced
        3 cups cubed cooked chicken
        2 cups (8 ounces) shredded cheddar cheese

In a large saucepan, melt butter; stir in flour and seasonings until smooth. Gradually add milk and cream. Bring to a boil; cook and stir for 2 minutes. Remove from the heat.

In a greased 13-in. x 9-in. x 2-in. baking dish, layer half of the noodles, avocados, chicken, white sauce and cheese. Repeat layers. Cover and bake at 350° for 20-25 minutes. Uncover; bake 5 minutes longer or until bubbly. **Yield:** 6 servings.

Turkey Florentine

This creamy dish is one of my family's favorite ways to use up leftover turkey and gravy. With the spinach and noodles, it's a hearty meal.
—Emily Chaney, Penobscot, Maine

        1 package (10 ounces) frozen chopped spinach
        2 tablespoons butter
        2 cups cooked noodles
    1-1/2 cups diced cooked turkey
        1 cup turkey *or* chicken gravy
        1 carton (8 ounces) sour cream onion dip
    1/2 teaspoon onion salt
        2 tablespoons grated Parmesan cheese

Cook the spinach according to package directions and drain. Stir in the butter. Place the noodles in a greased 11-in. x 7-in. x 2-in. baking dish; top with the spinach.

Combine turkey, gravy, onion dip and onion salt; spoon over spinach. Sprinkle with Parmesan. Bake, uncovered, at 325° for 25 minutes or until bubbly. **Yield:** 6 servings.

Crunchy Curried Chicken

If you have leftover ham and chicken (or turkey) on hand, try this. It's a great potluck dish because it can be made a day ahead. —Eleanor Doering
Stoughton, Wisconsin

4-1/2 cups cooked long grain rice
　1 cup cubed cooked chicken
　1 cup cubed fully cooked ham
　1 can (8 ounces) water chestnuts,
　　drained and chopped
　1 can (10-3/4 ounces) condensed cream of
　　chicken soup, undiluted
1-1/4 cups milk
　1/2 cup mayonnaise
　1/4 cup minced fresh parsley
　3/4 teaspoon salt
　1/8 to 1/4 teaspoon curry powder
　1/3 cup sliced almonds

Place the rice in a greased 13-in. x 9-in. x 2-in. baking dish. Sprinkle with the chicken, ham and water chestnuts. Combine the next six ingredients and pour over the chicken mixture. Bake, uncovered, at 350° for 30-35 minutes or until bubbly. Sprinkle with the almonds and bake 5 minutes longer. **Yield:** 6-8 servings.

Editor's Note: Reduced-fat or fat-free mayonnaise is not recommended for this recipe.

Wild Rice Turkey Dish

This rich, flavorful main dish has been one of my favorite meals to serve company. Made in one easy step, it's a real time-saver. Plus, it's a great way to use up leftover turkey. —Clara Sawlaw
Paris, Illinois

　6 cups cooked wild rice
　3 cups cubed cooked turkey
　1 can (10-3/4 ounces) condensed cream of
　　mushroom soup, undiluted
　3 celery ribs, sliced
1-1/3 cups sliced fresh mushrooms
　1 medium onion, chopped
　1 cup (8 ounces) sour cream
　1/2 cup butter, melted
　1 teaspoon salt
　1/4 teaspoon pepper

In a large bowl, combine all of the ingredients. Pour into a greased 13-in. x 9-in. x 2-in. baking dish. Cover and bake at 350° for 45 minutes. Uncover and bake 15 minutes longer or until lightly browned. **Yield:** 10 servings.

Chicken Biscuit Bake

(Pictured above right)

Golden biscuits cover this homespun dish laden with chicken, broccoli and cheese. It's then topped

with a celery seed mixture. My family requests this all-in-one dinner once a month. —Karen Weirick
Bourbon, Indiana

　1 can (10-3/4 ounces) condensed cream of
　　chicken soup, undiluted
2/3 cup mayonnaise
　2 to 3 teaspoons Worcestershire sauce
　4 cups cubed cooked chicken
　3 cups chopped broccoli, cooked
　1 medium onion, chopped
　1 cup (4 ounces) shredded cheddar
　　cheese
　2 tubes (12 ounces *each*) refrigerated
　　buttermilk biscuits
　2 eggs
1/2 cup sour cream
　2 teaspoons celery seed
　1 teaspoon salt

In a bowl, combine the soup, mayonnaise and Worcestershire sauce. Stir in chicken, broccoli and onion. Transfer to a greased 13-in. x 9-in. x 2-in. baking dish. Sprinkle with cheese. Cover and bake at 375° for 20 minutes.

Separate biscuits; cut each in half. Arrange, cut side down, over hot chicken mixture. In a bowl, combine remaining ingredients; pour over biscuits. Bake, uncovered, 20 minutes longer or until golden brown. **Yield:** 6-8 servings.

Editor's Note: Reduced-fat or fat-free mayonnaise is not recommended for this recipe.

sauce, salt and pepper; add to vegetables. Bring to a boil. Pour over the chicken. Cover and bake at 350° for 30 minutes. Sprinkle with corn. Bake 18-20 minutes longer or until chicken juices run clear and corn is tender. **Yield:** 4-6 servings.

Chicken Tortilla Bake

(Pictured below)

Mother frequently made this comforting casserole when I was growing up. Our family would scrape the pan clean. Chicken, cheese and zippy green chilies are a mouth-watering mix.   —Jerri Moror
Rio Rancho, New Mexico

  3 cups shredded cooked chicken
  2 cans (4 ounces *each*) chopped green
    chilies
  1 cup chicken broth
  1 can (10-3/4 ounces) condensed cream of
    mushroom soup, undiluted
  1 can (10-3/4 ounces) condensed cream of
    chicken soup, undiluted
  1 small onion, finely chopped
 12 corn tortillas
  2 cups (8 ounces) shredded cheddar
    cheese, *divided*

In a bowl, combine the chicken, chilies, broth, soups and onion; set aside. Warm tortillas in the microwave according to package directions. Layer half

Barbecue Chicken Casserole

(Pictured above)

I am a minister's wife and have cooked for countless fellowships, funeral dinners and other church activities. This is a recipe I've used often for those occasions.   —Gail Rector, Belle, Missouri

  1 cup all-purpose flour
  1 broiler/fryer chicken (3 to 4 pounds),
    cut up
  2 tablespoons vegetable oil
  1 cup chopped onion
  1 cup chopped green pepper
  1 cup thinly sliced celery
  1 cup ketchup
1/2 cup water
  3 tablespoons brown sugar
  3 tablespoons Worcestershire sauce
1/2 teaspoon salt
1/4 teaspoon pepper
  1 package (16 ounces) frozen corn,
    thawed

Place flour in a large resealable plastic bag. Add chicken, a few pieces at a time, and shake to coat. In a large skillet, brown the chicken in oil; transfer to an ungreased 13-in. x 9-in. x 2-in. baking dish. Drain skillet, reserving 2 tablespoons drippings.

In the drippings, saute onion, green pepper and celery until tender. In a bowl, combine the ketchup, water, brown sugar, Worcestershire

of the tortillas on the bottom of a greased 13-in. x 9-in. x 2-in. baking pan, cutting to fit pan if desired. Top with half of the chicken mixture and half of the cheese. Repeat layers. Bake, uncovered, at 350° for 30 minutes. **Yield:** 6-8 servings.

Chicken Hot Dish

When my brother and his wife came over to visit after our third child was born, they brought this comforting creamy dish for supper. It's become a favorite since then.
—Amber Dudley
New Prague, Minnesota

   1 package (26 ounces) frozen shredded
      hash brown potatoes, thawed
   1 package (24 ounces) frozen California-
      blend vegetables
   3 cups cubed cooked chicken
   1 can (10-3/4 ounces) condensed cream of
      chicken soup, undiluted
   1 can (10-3/4 ounces) condensed cream of
      mushroom soup, undiluted
   1 cup chicken broth
 3/4 cup french-fried onions

In a greased 13-in. x 9-in. x 2-in. baking dish, layer the potatoes, vegetables and chicken. In a bowl, combine soups and broth; pour over the chicken (dish will be full). Cover and bake at 375° for 1 hour. Uncover; sprinkle with onions. Bake 10 minutes longer or until heated through. **Yield:** 6 servings.

Crunchy Turkey Casserole

This comforting casserole is perfect for a family supper. It has an appealing crunch from water chestnuts, almonds and chow mein noodles.
—Lois Koogler, Sidney, Ohio

   2 cans (10-3/4 ounces *each*) condensed
      cream of mushroom soup, undiluted
 1/2 cup milk *or* chicken broth
   4 cups cubed cooked turkey
   2 celery ribs, thinly sliced
   1 small onion, chopped
   1 can (8 ounces) sliced water chestnuts,
      drained and halved
   1 tablespoon soy sauce
   1 can (3 ounces) chow mein noodles
 1/2 cup slivered almonds

In a large bowl, combine soup and milk. Stir in the turkey, celery, onion, water chestnuts and soy sauce. Transfer to a greased shallow 2-qt. baking

dish. Sprinkle with noodles and almonds. Bake, uncovered, at 350° for 30 minutes or until heated through. **Yield:** 6-8 servings.

Chicken Bean Casserole

(Pictured above)

I love to make this hearty casserole with crisp-tender green beans. A perfect use for leftover chicken, it makes a satisfying meal.
—Darlene Markel
Mt. Hood, Oregon

      6 tablespoons butter
      6 tablespoons all-purpose flour
 1-1/2 cups chicken broth
    1/2 cup milk
      1 to 2 teaspoons soy sauce
    1/2 teaspoon salt
 Dash pepper
    2/3 cup shredded Parmesan cheese, *divided*
      8 cups fresh cut green *or* wax beans,
         cooked and drained
      2 cups cubed cooked chicken

In a saucepan, melt butter. Stir in flour until smooth. Gradually add broth, milk, soy sauce, salt and pepper. Bring to a boil; cook and stir for 2 minutes or until thickened. Remove from the heat. Stir in 1/3 cup Parmesan cheese until melted. Add beans and chicken; toss to coat.

   Transfer to a greased 2-qt. baking dish; sprinkle with the remaining cheese. Bake, uncovered, at 375° for 15-18 minutes or until golden brown. **Yield:** 6-8 servings.

Turkey Broccoli Hollandaise

(Pictured below)

This dish is a great way to use extra turkey. The original recipe called for Thanksgiving leftovers, but my family loves it so much that I prepare it all year.
—Pamela Yoder, Elkhart, Indiana

1 cup fresh broccoli florets
1 package (6 ounces) stuffing mix
1 envelope hollandaise sauce mix
2 cups cubed cooked turkey *or* chicken
1 can (2.8 ounces) french-fried onions

Place 1 in. of water and broccoli in a saucepan. Bring to a boil. Reduce heat; cover and simmer for 5-8 minutes or until crisp-tender. Meanwhile, prepare stuffing and sauce mixes according to package directions.

Spoon stuffing into a greased 11-in. x 7-in. x 2-in. baking dish. Top with turkey. Drain broccoli; arrange over turkey. Spoon sauce over top; sprinkle with onions. Bake, uncovered, at 325° for 25-30 minutes or until heated through. **Yield:** 6 servings.

Chicken Noodle Casserole

(Pictured on page 34)

Everyone who tries this comforting combination asks for the recipe.
—Kay Pederson
Yellville, Arkansas

1 can (10-3/4 ounces) condensed cream of chicken soup, undiluted
1/2 cup mayonnaise
2 tablespoons lemon juice
2 cups cubed cooked chicken
1 small onion, chopped
1/4 cup chopped green pepper
1/4 cup chopped sweet red pepper
1 cup (4 ounces) shredded Monterey Jack cheese, *divided*
1 cup (4 ounces) shredded sharp cheddar cheese, *divided*
12 ounces medium egg noodles, cooked and drained

In a large bowl, combine soup, mayonnaise and lemon juice. Add the chicken, onion, peppers, 1/2 cup of Monterey Jack cheese and 1/2 cup of cheddar cheese; mix well. Add noodles and toss to coat.

Transfer to a greased 2-qt. baking dish. Bake, uncovered, at 350° for 30-35 minutes. Sprinkle with remaining cheeses. Bake 10 minutes longer or until vegetables are tender and cheese is melted. **Yield:** 6 servings.

Editor's Note: Reduced-fat or fat-free mayonnaise is not recommended for this recipe.

Corn Bread Turkey Casserole

Folks will appreciate the flavor and convenience of this casserole. The recipe makes three pans, so enjoy one for dinner and freeze the other two.
—Michelle Flynn, Philadelphia, Pennsylvania

3 packages (6 ounces *each*) crushed corn bread stuffing mix
10 to 11 cups cubed cooked turkey *or* chicken
2 cups (8 ounces) shredded cheddar cheese
2 cans (10-3/4 ounces *each*) condensed cream of celery soup, undiluted
2 cans (10-3/4 ounces *each*) condensed cream of chicken soup, undiluted
1 can (10-3/4 ounces) condensed cream of mushroom soup, undiluted
1 can (12 ounces) evaporated milk
1-1/2 cups (6 ounces) shredded Swiss cheese

Prepare stuffing mix according to package directions. Add turkey and cheddar cheese. Combine the soups and milk. Pour 1 cup each into three greased 13-in. x 9-in. x 2-in. baking dishes. Top each with turkey mixture and remaining soup mixture. Sprinkle with Swiss cheese.

Cover and freeze two casseroles for up to 3

months. Cover and bake the remaining casserole at 350° for 30-35 minutes or until bubbly. Let stand for 5-10 minutes before serving.

To use frozen casseroles: Thaw in refrigerator. Remove from refrigerator 30 minutes before baking. Bake, uncovered, at 350° for 35-40 minutes or until bubbly. Let stand 5-10 minutes before serving. **Yield:** 3 casseroles (8-10 servings each).

Oregano Turkey Casserole

This casserole is a great way to use up leftover turkey. The oregano really enhances its flavor.
—*Edie DeSpain, Logan, Utah*

    4 ounces uncooked spaghetti
    2 cups sliced fresh mushrooms
    1/2 cup julienned green pepper
    1/4 cup butter
    2 tablespoons all-purpose flour
    2 tablespoons minced fresh oregano
      or 2 teaspoons dried oregano
    1/2 teaspoon salt
    1/4 teaspoon pepper
    1 teaspoon chicken bouillon granules
    1/4 cup boiling water
  1-1/3 cups evaporated milk
  2-1/2 cups cubed cooked turkey
    2 tablespoons chopped pimientos
    2 tablespoons grated Parmesan cheese

Cook spaghetti according to package directions. Meanwhile, in a skillet, saute mushrooms and green pepper in butter until tender. Stir in flour, oregano, salt and pepper. Dissolve bouillon in water; gradually add to skillet. Stir in milk. Bring to a boil; cook and stir for 2 minutes or until thickened. Add turkey and pimientos.

Drain spaghetti; toss with the turkey mixture. Pour into a greased 11-in. x 7-in. x 2-in. baking dish. Sprinkle with Parmesan cheese. Bake, uncovered, at 350° for 18-22 minutes or until heated through. **Yield:** 6-8 servings.

Chicken 'n' Biscuits

(Pictured above right)

This cheesy chicken casserole gets its vibrant color from frozen vegetables and its unique flavor from crumbled bacon. The biscuit-topped dish has become a regular at our dinner table.
—*Debbie Vannette, Zeeland, Michigan*

    1 package (16 ounces) frozen mixed
      vegetables
  2-1/2 cups cubed cooked chicken
    1 can (10-3/4 ounces) condensed cream of
      chicken soup, undiluted
    3/4 cup milk
  1-1/2 cups (6 ounces) shredded cheddar
      cheese, *divided*
    8 bacon strips, cooked and crumbled,
      optional
BISCUITS:
  1-1/2 cups biscuit/baking mix
    2/3 cup milk
    1 can (2.8 ounces) french-fried onions

In a large bowl, combine the vegetables, chicken, soup, milk, 1 cup cheese and bacon if desired. Pour into an ungreased 13-in. x 9-in. x 2-in. baking dish. Cover and bake at 400° for 15 minutes.

Meanwhile, in another bowl, combine biscuit mix and milk. Drop batter by tablespoonfuls onto chicken mixture. Bake, uncovered, for 20-22 minutes or until biscuits are golden brown. Top with onions and remaining cheese. Bake 3-4 minutes longer or until cheese is melted. **Yield:** 6 servings.

Chicken Clue

Keep a package of frozen cubed cooked chicken from the freezer section of your supermarket on hand for those days when you're in a hurry to put together a casserole. Or use cans of boneless chunk chicken.

Chicken Veggie Casserole

(Pictured above)

This is a hot, satisfying complete meal in one dish. It's easy on me and enjoyed by my family.
—*Martha Balser, Cincinnati, Ohio*

> 1 can (10-3/4 ounces) condensed cream of chicken soup, undiluted
> 1/2 cup milk
> 1/4 teaspoon dried thyme
> 1/4 teaspoon salt
> 1/4 teaspoon pepper
> 2 cups diced cooked chicken
> 1 can (16 ounces) whole kernel corn, drained
> 2 cups frozen cut green beans, thawed
> 2 cups sliced cooked potatoes

In a large bowl, combine the soup, milk, thyme, salt and pepper. Stir in chicken, corn, beans and potatoes. Pour into a greased 1-1/2-qt. baking dish. Bake, uncovered, at 400° for 15 minutes or until heated through. **Yield:** 6 servings.

Chicken 'n' Chips

(Pictured at right)

My husband, Chad, is always ready to try a new recipe, so I surprised him with this creamy chicken casserole sprinkled with crushed tortilla chips.

He loves the flavor, and I like that it's the perfect size for our small family. —*Kendra Schneider Grifton, North Carolina*

> 1 can (10-3/4 ounces) condensed cream of chicken soup, undiluted
> 1 cup (8 ounces) sour cream
> 2 tablespoons taco sauce
> 1/4 cup chopped green chilies
> 3 cups cubed cooked chicken
> 12 slices process American cheese
> 4 cups broken tortilla chips

In a bowl, combine the soup, sour cream, taco sauce and chilies. In an ungreased shallow 2-qt. baking dish, layer half of the chicken, soup mixture, cheese and tortilla chips. Repeat layers. Bake, uncovered, at 350° for 25-30 minutes or until bubbly. **Yield:** 4-6 servings.

Scalloped Chicken Casserole

This is a great catchall casserole. Any meat can be used, and vegetables may be substituted based on what you have available. —*Marion White La Center, Washington*

> 1 cup chopped green onions
> 1 cup chopped celery
> 1 small green *or* sweet red pepper, chopped

1/2 cup shredded carrots
2 garlic cloves, minced
2 tablespoons vegetable oil
2 cups cubed cooked chicken
1 cup (4 ounces) shredded cheddar
  cheese
1 cup (4 ounces) shredded mozzarella
  cheese
1/2 cup mayonnaise
1 tablespoon minced fresh parsley
  or 1 teaspoon dried parsley flakes
14 slices day-old whole wheat bread, cubed
4 eggs
2 cups milk
1 can (10-3/4 ounces) condensed cream of
  chicken soup, undiluted
1 tablespoon Worcestershire sauce
Paprika

In a skillet, saute onions, celery, green pepper, carrots and garlic in oil until crisp-tender. Transfer to a large bowl; add chicken, cheeses, mayonnaise and parsley. Place half of the bread cubes in a greased 13-in. x 9-in. x 2-in. baking dish. Top with chicken mixture and remaining bread.

In a bowl, beat eggs; add milk, soup and Worcestershire sauce. Pour over casserole. Sprinkle with paprika. Bake, uncovered, at 350° for 1 hour and 10 minutes or until a knife inserted near the center comes out clean. **Yield:** 12-16 servings.

Editor's Note: Reduced-fat or fat-free mayonnaise is not recommended for this recipe.

Bring to a boil; cook and stir for 2 minutes. Stir in turkey and peas. Transfer to a greased 13-in. x 9-in. x 2-in. baking dish. Separate biscuits and arrange over the top. Sprinkle with cheese. Bake, uncovered, at 425° for 17-20 minutes or until golden brown. **Yield:** 4-6 servings.

Creamy Turkey and Biscuits

This recipe turns leftover holiday turkey into a quick, comforting casserole that gets plenty of appeal when topped with refrigerator biscuits.
  —Annette Gorton, Miles City, Montana

1/3 cup chopped green pepper
1/3 cup chopped onion
3 tablespoons butter
1/4 cup biscuit/baking mix
1-1/2 cups milk
1 can (10-3/4 ounces) condensed cream of
  mushroom soup, undiluted
2 cups cubed cooked turkey
1 cup frozen peas
2 tubes (7-1/2 ounces *each*) refrigerated
  buttermilk biscuits
3/4 cup shredded cheddar cheese

In a large saucepan, saute green pepper and onion in butter until tender. Stir in biscuit mix until blended. Gradually add milk and soup; stir until blended.

Chicken Stir-Fry Bake

(Pictured above)

One night, while trying to tend to both dinner and our son, I used frozen vegetables in my chicken stir-fry. Not wanting to stand watch over the stovetop, I baked the entree. Guests say it tastes like it's hot from the skillet. —Carly Carter, Nashville, Tennessee

2 cups uncooked instant rice
1 can (8 ounces) sliced water chestnuts,
  drained
2 cups cubed cooked chicken
1 package (16 ounces) frozen stir-fry
  vegetables, thawed
1 can (14-1/2 ounces) chicken broth
1/4 cup soy sauce
1 garlic clove, minced
1/2 to 3/4 teaspoon ground ginger

Place rice in an 11-in. x 7-in. x 2-in. baking dish. Layer with water chestnuts, chicken and vegetables. Combine the remaining ingredients; pour over chicken and vegetables. Cover and bake at 375° for 25 minutes or until rice is tender. **Yield:** 4 servings.

Cashew Chicken Casserole

(Pictured below)

I especially like this dish because I can get it ready the day before I need it. It's easy to whip up with common pantry items, including macaroni, canned soup and saltine crackers.
—Julie Ridlon
Solway, Minnesota

    2 cups uncooked elbow macaroni
    3 cups cubed cooked chicken
  1/2 cup cubed process American cheese
    1 small onion, chopped
  1/2 cup chopped celery
  1/2 cup chopped green pepper
    1 can (8 ounces) sliced water chestnuts, drained
    1 can (10-3/4 ounces) condensed cream of mushroom soup, undiluted
    1 can (10-3/4 ounces) condensed cream of chicken soup, undiluted
1-1/3 cups milk
    1 can (14-1/2 ounces) chicken broth
  1/4 cup butter, melted
  2/3 cup crushed saltines (about 20 crackers)
  3/4 cup cashew halves

In a greased 13-in. x 9-in. x 2-in. baking dish, layer the first seven ingredients in the order listed above. In a bowl, combine the soups, milk and broth. Pour over the top of the water chestnuts. Cover and re-frigerate overnight.

Toss butter and cracker crumbs; sprinkle over casserole. Top with cashews. Bake, uncovered, at 350° for 35-40 minutes or until macaroni is tender. **Yield:** 6 servings.

Chicken Artichoke Casserole

This creamy chicken dish is so easy to prepare that it's perfect for serving to guests.   *—Diane Hixon*
Niceville, Florida

    1 pound boneless skinless chicken breasts, cut into 2-inch cubes
    4 tablespoons butter, *divided*
Salt and pepper to taste
    1 package (9 ounces) frozen artichoke hearts, thawed *or* 1 can (14 ounces) water-packed artichoke hearts, drained and halved
  1/4 cup all-purpose flour
  1/8 teaspoon ground nutmeg
    2 cups chicken broth
    1 cup (4 ounces) shredded cheddar cheese
  1/4 cup dry bread crumbs
    1 tablespoon minced fresh savory *or* 1 teaspoon dried savory
    1 tablespoon minced fresh thyme *or* 1 teaspoon dried thyme
Hot cooked noodles *or* rice

In a skillet, saute chicken in 1 tablespoon butter until no longer pink. Season with salt and pepper. Place chicken and artichokes in a greased 11-in. x 7-in. x 2-in. baking dish; set aside.

In a saucepan, melt remaining butter; stir in flour and nutmeg until smooth. Gradually add broth. Bring to a boil; cook and stir for 2 minutes or until thickened and bubbly. Stir in cheese until melted; spoon over chicken.

Combine bread crumbs, savory and thyme; sprinkle over chicken. Bake, uncovered, at 350° for 25-35 minutes or until golden brown. Serve over noodles or rice. **Yield:** 4-6 servings.

Onion-Chicken Stuffing Bake

A friend shared this savory meal-in-one with me, and it's since become my favorite dinner to serve guests. It's sure to be a hit at your home, too.
—Audrey Aldrich, Berlin Heights, Ohio

1 package (6 ounces) seasoned stuffing
  mix
3 cups cubed cooked chicken
1 can (10-3/4 ounces) condensed cream of
  chicken soup, undiluted
1 cup (8 ounces) sour cream
2 tablespoons onion soup mix
1 can (4 ounces) mushroom stems and
  pieces, drained
1 can (8 ounces) sliced water chestnuts,
  drained
1/4 cup grated Parmesan cheese

Prepare stuffing mix according to package directions; set aside. Place chicken in a greased 2-qt. baking dish. Combine the soup, sour cream and soup mix; spread over the chicken.

Sprinkle with mushrooms and water chestnuts. Spread stuffing over top. Sprinkle with Parmesan cheese. Bake, uncovered, at 350° for 30-35 minutes or until bubbly. **Yield:** 6-8 servings.

Turkey Asparagus Casserole

It takes just minutes to assemble this creamy casserole. Convenient frozen asparagus lends bright color and garden flavor while a sprinkling of french-fried onion rings provides a yummy crunch.
—Cheryl Schut, Grand Rapids, Michigan

1 package (8 ounces) frozen chopped
  asparagus
2 cups cubed cooked turkey *or* chicken
1 can (10-3/4 ounces) condensed cream of
  chicken soup, undiluted
1/4 cup water
1 can (2.8 ounces) french-fried onions

In a small saucepan, cook asparagus in a small amount of water for 2 minutes; drain. Place in a greased 11-in. x 7-in. x 2-in. baking dish. Top with turkey. Combine soup and water; spoon over turkey. Bake, uncovered, at 350° for 25-30 minutes. Sprinkle with onions. Bake 5 minutes longer or until golden brown. **Yield:** 4 servings.

Turkey Tetrazzini

(Pictured above right)

This is a tasty main dish and a great way to use leftover chicken or turkey. Everyone loves the spaghetti noodles mixed in. —Sue Ross
Casa Grande, Arizona

2 cups broken uncooked spaghetti (2-inch
  pieces)
1 chicken bouillon cube
3/4 cup boiling water
1 can (10-3/4 ounces) condensed cream of
  mushroom soup, undiluted
1/8 teaspoon celery salt
1/8 teaspoon pepper
1-1/2 cups cubed cooked turkey
1 small onion, finely chopped
2 tablespoons diced pimientos, drained
1-1/2 cups (6 ounces) shredded cheddar
  cheese, *divided*

Cook spaghetti according to package directions. Meanwhile, in a bowl, dissolve bouillon in water. Add soup, celery salt and pepper. Drain spaghetti; add to soup mixture. Stir in turkey, onion, pimientos and 1/2 cup of cheese.

Transfer to a greased 8-in. square baking dish. Top with remaining cheese. Bake, uncovered, at 350° for 35-40 minutes or until heated through. **Yield:** 6 servings.

Best Baking Dishes

Casseroles are best cooked in baking dishes made of oven-safe glass or ceramic. Metal pans may discolor if the ingredients are acidic or may give off a metallic flavor.

in. baking dish. Combine topping ingredients; sprinkle over turkey mixture. Bake, uncovered, at 350° for 35-40 minutes or until bubbly and golden brown. **Yield:** 8-10 servings.

Editor's Note: Reduced-fat or fat-free mayonnaise is not recommended for this recipe.

Pecan Chicken Casserole

(Pictured below)

I got this recipe from a radio show years ago. It's one of my favorites. —Jackie Heyer, Cushing, Iowa

        1 cup all-purpose flour
        1 cup (4 ounces) finely shredded cheddar
            cheese
    3/4 cup finely chopped pecans
    1/2 teaspoon salt
    1/4 teaspoon paprika
    1/3 cup vegetable oil
FILLING:
        4 eggs
        1 cup (8 ounces) sour cream
        1 cup chicken broth
        4 cups diced cooked chicken
    1/2 cup finely shredded cheddar cheese
    1/4 cup finely chopped onion
    1/4 cup mayonnaise
    1/4 teaspoon dill seed
    1/8 teaspoon hot pepper sauce

Almond Turkey Casserole

(Pictured above)

A special cousin shared the recipe for this comforting casserole. The almonds and water chestnuts give it a fun crunch.   —Jill Black, Troy, Ontario

        2 cans (10-3/4 ounces *each*) condensed
            cream of mushroom soup, undiluted
    1/2 cup mayonnaise
    1/2 cup sour cream
        2 tablespoons chopped onion
        2 tablespoons lemon juice
        1 teaspoon salt
    1/2 teaspoon white pepper
        5 cups cubed cooked turkey
        3 cups cooked rice
        4 celery ribs, chopped
        1 can (8 ounces) sliced water chestnuts,
            drained
        1 cup sliced almonds
TOPPING:
1-1/2 cups crushed butter-flavored crackers
            (about 38 crackers)
    1/3 cup butter, melted
    1/4 cup sliced almonds

In a large bowl, combine the soup, mayonnaise, sour cream, onion, lemon juice, salt and pepper. Stir in the turkey, rice, celery, water chestnuts and almonds. Transfer to a greased 13-in. x 9-in. x 2-

In a bowl, combine the first six ingredients. Set aside 1/2 cup of crumb mixture for topping. Press remaining crumb mixture onto the bottom of a greased 13-in. x 9-in. x 2-in. baking dish. (Crust will be crumbly.) Bake at 350° for 10 minutes or until lightly browned.

In a bowl, beat eggs. Add the remaining ingredients. Pour over baked crust. Sprinkle with reserved crumb mixture. Bake at 350° for 25-30 minutes or until a knife inserted near the center comes out clean. Let stand for 10 minutes before cutting. **Yield:** 12 servings.

Editor's Note: Reduced-fat or fat-free mayonnaise is not recommended for this recipe.

Turkey Enchilada Casserole

This is a hearty satisfying entree that calls for ground turkey instead of the usual ground beef. We like the zippy flavor of the dish.
—Marcia Schmiedt, Anchorage, Alaska

1 pound ground turkey
1-1/2 cups chopped onions
2 garlic cloves, minced
1 tablespoon plus 1/3 cup vegetable oil, *divided*
1/3 cup all-purpose flour
2 tablespoons chili powder
3/4 teaspoon seasoned salt
1/8 teaspoon pepper
4 cups water
12 corn tortillas (7 inches)
1-1/2 cups (6 ounces) shredded cheddar cheese
1-1/2 cups salsa

In a skillet over medium heat, cook turkey, onions and garlic in 1 tablespoon oil until meat is no longer pink; drain. Sprinkle with flour, chili powder, seasoned salt and pepper. Add water; bring to a boil. Reduce heat; simmer, uncovered, for 8-10 minutes or until reduced.

In another skillet, fry tortillas in remaining oil for about 15 seconds, turning once. Drain well. Cut nine tortillas in half. Place cut edge of one tortilla against each short side of a greased 11-in. x 7-in. x 2-in. baking dish. Place cut edge of two tortillas against long sides of dish, overlapping to fit. Place a whole tortilla in center.

Spoon 2 cups of meat mixture over tortillas; sprinkle with 1/2 cup cheese. Repeat layers. Top with the remaining tortillas and meat sauce. Bake, uncovered, at 375° for 20 minutes. Sprinkle with the remaining cheese. Bake 5-10 minutes longer or until the cheese is melted. Serve with salsa. **Yield:** 8 servings.

Turkey Sausage and Noodles

(Pictured above)

During the winter months when our appetites are in full gear, my family practically licks this pan clean. I sometimes toss in a can of white kidney beans to make it even heartier.
—Helen Wanamaker Vail
Glenside, Pennsylvania

2 cups uncooked egg noodles
2 pounds Italian turkey sausage, cut into 1-inch slices
1 large onion, chopped
2 medium carrots, sliced
1/2 cup chopped green pepper
1/2 cup all-purpose flour
2-1/2 cups milk
1/4 cup Worcestershire sauce
1/4 teaspoon rubbed sage

Cook noodles according to package directions; drain. In a large skillet, cook sausage, onion, carrots and green pepper over medium heat until meat is no longer pink and carrots are crisp-tender. Stir in flour until blended. Gradually add milk. Bring to a boil; cook and stir for 2 minutes or until thickened. Stir in the noodles, Worcestershire sauce and sage.

Transfer to a greased 2-1/2-qt. baking dish. Cover; bake at 350° for 20 minutes. Uncover; bake 10-15 minutes longer or until bubbly. **Yield:** 8 servings.

Ravioli Chicken Casserole

I threw this together one evening when I had to work late and my new in-laws stopped over for the first time. —Stacie Knackmuhs
Decatur, Illinois

1 package (24 ounces) frozen cheese
  ravioli, cooked and drained
3 cups cubed cooked chicken
6 medium fresh mushrooms, sliced
1/2 cup chopped green pepper
1/3 cup chopped onion
1 jar (28 ounces) meatless spaghetti
  sauce
2 cups (8 ounces) shredded mozzarella
  cheese

In a greased 13-in. x 9-in. x 2-in. baking dish, layer the ravioli and chicken. Top with mushrooms, green pepper, onion and spaghetti sauce.

Cover and bake at 350° for 20 minutes. Uncover; sprinkle with cheese. Bake 10-15 minutes longer or until cheese is melted. **Yield:** 10-12 servings.

Turkey Potato Tetrazzini

(Pictured below)

This dish features layers of sliced potatoes, cooked turkey, broccoli and Swiss cheese with creamy Alfredo sauce spooned over it all. —Karen Bundy
Cabot, Pennsylvania

1 jar (16 ounces) Alfredo sauce
1 cup milk

Scalloped Chicken Supper

(Pictured above)

Canned soup and a package of scalloped potato mix hurry along this creamy and comforting casserole. You can use either leftover chicken or turkey with delicious results. —Cheryl Maczko
Arthurdale, West Virginia

1 package (4.9 ounces) scalloped
  potatoes
1/8 teaspoon poultry seasoning
1-3/4 cups boiling water
1 can (10-3/4 ounces) condensed cream
  of chicken soup, undiluted
2 cups cubed cooked chicken
1 cup shredded carrots
1/2 cup chopped celery
1/4 cup finely chopped onion

Set the potatoes aside. Place the contents of the sauce mix in a large bowl; sprinkle with poultry seasoning. Whisk in the water and soup. Stir in the chicken, carrots, celery, onion and potatoes.

Transfer to a greased 2-qt. baking dish. Bake, uncovered, at 400° for 45-50 minutes or until vegetables are tender. **Yield:** 4 servings.

7 medium potatoes, peeled and thinly
   sliced
4 tablespoons grated Parmesan cheese,
   divided
1-1/2 cups diced cooked turkey *or* chicken
2 cups (8 ounces) shredded Swiss
   cheese, *divided*
1 package (10 ounces) frozen chopped
   broccoli, thawed

In a bowl, combine Alfredo sauce and milk; spread
1/4 cup into a greased 13-in. x 9-in. x 2-in. baking
dish. Top with a third of the potatoes; sprinkle with
1 tablespoon Parmesan cheese.

In a bowl, combine the turkey, 1-1/2 cups Swiss
cheese and broccoli; spoon about 2 cups over potatoes. Top with about 2/3 cup sauce mixture. Repeat layers twice.

Cover and bake at 400° for 45 minutes. Top
with remaining cheeses (dish will be full). Bake, uncovered, 20-25 minutes longer or until potatoes are
tender. Let stand for 5 minutes before serving.
Yield: 12-15 servings.

Chicken Zucchini Casserole

*A co-worker shared this recipe, which was origi-
nally her grandmother's. When I make it, I use a box
of refrigerated cooked chicken and fresh zucchini
my neighbor gives me from his garden.*
                  —Bev Dutro, Dayton, Ohio

1 package (6 ounces) stuffing mix
3/4 cup butter, melted
3 cups diced zucchini
2 cups cubed cooked chicken
1 can (10-3/4 ounces) condensed cream
   of chicken soup, undiluted
1 medium carrot, shredded
1/2 cup chopped onion
1/2 cup sour cream

In a large bowl, combine stuffing mix and butter. Set
aside 1/2 cup for topping. Add the zucchini, chick-
en, soup, carrot, onion and sour cream to the remaining stuffing mixture.

Transfer to a greased 2-qt. baking dish. Sprinkle
with reserved stuffing mixture. Bake, uncovered,

On the Side

A garden-fresh mixed green salad is the
perfect side dish to serve with a hearty
casserole. So is fresh bread.

at 350° for 40-45 minutes or until golden brown and
bubbly. **Yield:** 6 servings.

Turkey Taco Bake

(Pictured above)

*This is a great way to use up leftover turkey. It is
chock-full of popular south-of-the-border ingredients including corn chips, salsa and refried beans.*
           —Trudie Hagen, Roggen, Colorado

2 cups coarsely crushed corn chips
1 can (16 ounces) refried beans
2 cups (8 ounces) shredded Monterey
   Jack cheese, *divided*
1 cup salsa
2 cups shredded cooked turkey
1 teaspoon Mexican *or* taco seasoning
1 green onion, sliced
1 medium tomato, chopped

Place the corn chips in a greased shallow
2-1/2-qt. baking dish. Place the refried beans in a
small saucepan; cook and stir over medium heat
until heated through. Remove from the heat; stir in
1 cup cheese and salsa. Spread over chips.

Toss the turkey and Mexican seasoning; sprinkle over bean mixture. Top with remaining cheese.
Sprinkle with onion. Bake, uncovered, at 400° for
20-25 minutes or until cheese is melted. Sprinkle
with tomato. **Yield:** 4 servings.

Pork

Brat 'n' Tot Bake, p. 56

Chapter 4

Ham-It-Up Spaghetti

(Pictured below)

I found this recipe in a church cookbook I bought while touring the New England states. With its easy sauce and hearty chunks of ham, this casserole has become a family favorite. Using common ingredients, it's easy to assemble, especially when you cook the spaghetti while mixing up the remaining ingredients.
—Donna Gonda
North Canton, Ohio

- 1 package (16 ounces) spaghetti, broken into 2-inch pieces
- 2 cans (10-3/4 ounces *each*) condensed cream of mushroom soup, undiluted
- 1-3/4 cups milk
- 1 tablespoon dried minced onion
- 2 teaspoons dried parsley flakes
- 1 teaspoon Worcestershire sauce
- 2 cups cubed fully cooked ham (about 1 pound)
- 2 cups (8 ounces) shredded cheddar cheese

Cook spaghetti according to package directions. Meanwhile, in a large bowl, combine soup, milk, onion, parsley and Worcestershire sauce. Drain spaghetti; add to soup mixture with ham.

Transfer to a lightly greased 2-1/2-qt. baking dish. Sprinkle with cheese. Cover and bake at 375°

for 15 minutes. Uncover and bake 5 minutes longer or until lightly browned and heated through. **Yield:** 6-8 servings.

Sausage Spaghetti Spirals

My family loves this flavorful casserole with hearty chunks of sausage and green pepper. The recipe makes a big pan, so it's nicely sized for a potluck.
—Carol Carlton, Wheaton, Illinois

✓ Uses less fat, sugar or salt. Includes Nutritional Analysis and Diabetic Exchanges.

- 1 pound bulk Italian sausage
- 1 medium green pepper, chopped
- 5 cups spiral pasta, cooked and drained
- 1 jar (28 ounces) meatless spaghetti sauce
- 1-1/2 cups (6 ounces) shredded mozzarella cheese

In a skillet, cook sausage and green pepper over medium heat until meat is no longer pink; drain. Stir in pasta and spaghetti sauce; mix well. Transfer to a greased 13-in. x 9-in. x 2-in. baking dish. Cover and bake at 350° for 25 minutes. Uncover; sprinkle with cheese. Bake 5-10 minutes longer or until the cheese is melted. **Yield:** 10 servings.

Nutritional Analysis: One 1-cup serving (prepared with turkey Italian sausage and reduced-fat mozzarella) equals 249 calories, 8 g fat (3 g saturated fat), 34 mg cholesterol, 710 mg sodium, 28 g carbohydrate, 2 g fiber, 16 g protein. **Diabetic Exchanges:** 2 starch, 1-1/2 lean meat.

Hearty Barley Bake

Barley is a nice change of pace from the usual pasta or rice in this colorful casserole. It's chock-full of spicy sausage and a variety of vegetables including spinach, carrots and corn.
—Jenny Browning, Cypress, Texas

- 2 cups sliced fresh mushrooms
- 1 cup thinly sliced carrots
- 1/2 cup chopped onion
- 1 garlic clove, minced
- 2 teaspoons vegetable oil
- 12 ounces bulk pork sausage
- 1-1/2 cups cooked medium pearl barley
- 1 can (14-3/4 ounces) cream-style corn
- 1 package (10 ounces) frozen chopped spinach, thawed and drained
- 3 green onions, sliced
- 1 teaspoon dried savory

1 teaspoon dried thyme
1/2 teaspoon dried marjoram
1/8 teaspoon pepper
1/2 cup shredded Parmesan cheese

In a skillet, saute mushrooms, carrots, onion and garlic in oil until tender; remove to a large bowl. In the same skillet, cook sausage over medium heat until no longer pink; drain. Add to mushroom mixture. Add barley, corn, spinach, onions, savory, thyme, marjoram and pepper; mix well.

Transfer to a greased shallow 2-qt. baking dish. Cover; bake at 350° for 40 minutes. Sprinkle with cheese. Bake, uncovered, 5 minutes longer or until cheese is melted. **Yield:** 6 servings.

Scalloped Potatoes 'n' Franks

This kid-pleasing combination was requested often when our children were young. Now that they're grown, they like to make it for their families because it doesn't require any fancy ingredients.
—Sandra Scheirer, Mertztown, Pennsylvania

2 tablespoons chopped onion
3 tablespoons butter
1/4 cup all-purpose flour
1-1/2 teaspoons salt
1/8 teaspoon pepper
2 cups milk
1 cup (4 ounces) shredded Swiss cheese
2 tablespoons minced fresh parsley
5 medium potatoes, peeled and thinly sliced
8 hot dogs, halved and sliced

In a saucepan, saute onion in butter until tender. Stir in flour, salt and pepper until blended. Gradually add milk. Bring to a boil over medium heat; cook and stir for 2 minutes. Remove from the heat; stir in cheese until melted. Add parsley.

Place half of potatoes in a greased 2-qt. baking dish; top with half of sauce. Arrange hot dogs over sauce. Top with remaining potatoes and sauce. Cover and bake at 350° for 1-1/2 hours or until bubbly. Uncover and bake 10 minutes longer or until lightly browned. **Yield:** 4-6 servings.

Colorful Pasta with Ham

(Pictured above right)

I made up this hearty noodle casserole as I went along, and my family was pleased with the end re-sult. I double the rapid recipe and store the extra casserole in the freezer for a night when time is at a premium. —Heather Rowan, Richmond, Missouri

1 package (16 ounces) tricolor spiral pasta
1-1/2 cups cubed fully cooked ham
1 can (15-1/4 ounces) whole kernel corn, drained
1-1/2 cups (6 ounces) shredded cheddar cheese, *divided*
1 can (2.8 ounces) french-fried onions, *divided*
1 can (14-1/2 ounces) chicken broth
1 can (10-3/4 ounces) condensed cream of chicken soup, undiluted
1/2 cup milk
1/2 teaspoon *each* celery salt, garlic powder and pepper

Cook pasta according to package directions; drain. In a greased shallow 3-qt. baking dish, combine the pasta, ham, corn, 1 cup cheese and 3/4 cup onions. In a bowl, combine the broth, soup, milk and seasonings. Pour over pasta mixture; mix well.

Bake, uncovered, at 350° for 30 minutes. Sprinkle with remaining cheese and onions. Bake 5 minutes longer or until heated through. **Yield:** 8 servings.

Got Leftovers?

Leftover pork dishes should be refrigerated within 2 hours of cooking and used within 2 days.

ing dish. Cover and bake at 350° for 40 minutes. Toss bread crumbs and butter; sprinkle over rice mixture. Bake, uncovered, for 10-15 minutes or until rice is tender. Let stand 10 minutes before serving. **Yield:** 12-14 servings.

Baked Rice with Sausage

(Pictured above)

This recipe is perfect for potlucks or church suppers since it produces a big batch and has flavors with broad appeal. Most folks can't guess that the secret ingredient is chicken noodle soup mix.
—Naomi Flood, Emporia, Kansas

2 pounds bulk Italian sausage
4 celery ribs, thinly sliced
1 large onion, chopped
1 large green pepper, chopped
4-1/2 cups water
3/4 cup dry chicken noodle soup mix (1-1/2 envelopes)
1 can (10-3/4 ounces) condensed cream of chicken soup, undiluted
1 cup uncooked long grain rice
1/4 cup dry bread crumbs
2 tablespoons butter, melted

In a large skillet, cook sausage, celery, onion and green pepper over medium heat until meat is no longer pink and vegetables are tender; drain. In a large saucepan, bring water to a boil; add dry soup mix. Reduce heat; simmer, uncovered, for 5 minutes or until the noodles are tender. Stir in canned soup, rice and sausage mixture; mix well.
Transfer to a greased 13-in. x 9-in. x 2-in. bak-

Scalloped Potatoes With Ham

(Pictured below)

This dish is a crowd-pleaser with its creamy sauce, chunks of ham and potato slices. I always enjoyed it when Mother made it. I add parsley and thyme, and now my husband and five children request it.
—Wendy Rhoades, Yacolt, Washington

6 tablespoons butter, *divided*
1/4 cup all-purpose flour
1 teaspoon dried parsley flakes
1 teaspoon salt
1/2 teaspoon dried thyme
1/4 teaspoon pepper
3 cups milk
6 cups thinly sliced peeled potatoes
1-1/2 cups chopped fully cooked ham
1 small onion, grated

In a saucepan, melt 4 tablespoons butter. Stir in flour, parsley, salt, thyme and pepper until smooth.

Gradually add milk; bring to a boil. Cook and stir for 2 minutes. Combine potatoes, ham and onion; place half in a greased 2-1/2-qt. baking dish. Top with half of the sauce; repeat layers.

Cover and bake at 375° for 65-75 minutes or until potatoes are almost tender. Dot with remaining butter. Bake, uncovered, 15-20 minutes longer or until potatoes are tender. **Yield:** 4 servings.

Pork Sauerkraut Casserole

I get lots of compliments on this tangy pork dish, so I fix it often. To speed preparation, I use frozen hash brown potatoes instead of peeling and slicing potatoes.
—Anne Yaeger, Houston, Texas

    1 can (27 ounces) sauerkraut, drained
    4 cups frozen cubed hash brown
      potatoes, thawed
    6 pork chops (1 inch thick)
    1 can (10-3/4 ounces) condensed tomato
      soup, undiluted
    1 medium onion, chopped
  1/2 cup water
  1/4 cup packed brown sugar
    2 tablespoons vinegar

In an ungreased 13-in. x 9-in. x 2-in. baking dish, combine sauerkraut and hash browns. Top with pork chops. Combine soup, onion, water, sugar and vinegar; pour over all. Bake, uncovered, at 350° for 1-1/2 hours. **Yield:** 6 servings.

Barbecued Pork And Beans

Everyone always raves about how tender these pork chops are.
—Donna Jordan
Hendersonville, North Carolina

    4 bone-in pork loin chops (3/4 inch thick)
    1 tablespoon vegetable oil
    2 cans (11 ounces each) pork and beans
    3 tablespoons Worcestershire sauce,
      divided
  1/4 cup ketchup
  1/4 to 1/2 teaspoon chili powder

In a large skillet, brown pork chops in oil on both sides. Combine pork and beans and 2 tablespoons Worcestershire sauce; place in a greased 11-in. x 7-in. x 2-in. baking dish. Top with chops.

Combine the ketchup, chili powder and remaining Worcestershire sauce; spoon over chops. Bake, uncovered, at 350° for 50-55 minutes or until meat is tender. **Yield:** 4 servings.

Pork and Green Chili Casserole

(Pictured above)

This zippy casserole is one that was brought to a picnic at my house. People raved over it.
—Dianne Esposite, New Middletown, Ohio

1-1/2 pounds boneless pork, cut into 1/2-inch
      cubes
    1 tablespoon vegetable oil
    1 can (15 ounces) black beans, rinsed and
      drained
    1 can (10-3/4 ounces) condensed cream of
      chicken soup, undiluted
    1 can (14-1/2 ounces) diced tomatoes,
      undrained
    2 cans (4 ounces *each*) chopped green
      chilies
    1 cup quick-cooking brown rice
  1/4 cup water
    2 to 3 tablespoons salsa
    1 teaspoon ground cumin
  1/2 cup shredded cheddar cheese

In a large skillet, saute pork in oil until no pink remains; drain. Add the beans, soup, tomatoes, chilies, rice, water, salsa and cumin; cook and stir until bubbly. Pour into an ungreased 2-qt. baking dish. Bake, uncovered, at 350° for 30 minutes or until bubbly. Sprinkle with cheese; let stand a few minutes before serving. **Yield:** 6 servings.

French Country Casserole

(Pictured below)

This delicious dish is great for busy nights when you don't have much time to devote to dinner. It's a quick-to-fix version of a traditional French cassoulet that was an instant hit with my husband.
—Kim Lowe, Coralville, Iowa

✓ Uses less fat, sugar or salt. Includes Nutritional Analysis and Diabetic Exchanges.

- **1 pound fully cooked kielbasa *or* Polish sausage, halved and cut into 1/4-inch slices**
- **1 can (16 ounces) kidney beans, rinsed and drained**
- **1 can (15-1/2 ounces) great northern beans, rinsed and drained**
- **1 can (15 ounces) black beans, rinsed and drained**
- **1 can (15 ounces) tomato sauce**
- **3 medium carrots, thinly sliced**
- **2 small onions, sliced into rings**
- **1/2 cup red wine *or* beef broth**
- **2 tablespoons brown sugar**
- **2 garlic cloves, minced**
- **1-1/2 teaspoons dried thyme**

Combine all ingredients in a bowl; transfer to an ungreased 3-qt. baking dish. Cover and bake at 375° for 60-70 minutes or until the carrots are tender. **Yield:** 9 servings.

Nutritional Analysis: One 1-cup serving (prepared with reduced-fat turkey kielbasa and reduced-sodium broth) equals 268 calories, 894 mg sodium, 33 mg cholesterol, 39 g carbohydrate, 19 g protein, 5 g fat. **Diabetic Exchanges:** 2 starch, 2 vegetable, 1-1/2 lean meat.

Brat 'n' Tot Bake

(Pictured on page 50)

As a volunteer at our annual Bratwurst Festival, I could not have someone in my family who disliked bratwurst, so I developed this cheesy casserole for our son. It's the only way he will eat them.
—Jodi Gobrecht, Bucyrus, Ohio

- **1 pound uncooked bratwurst, casings removed**
- **1 medium onion, chopped**
- **1 can (10-3/4 ounces) condensed cream of mushroom soup, undiluted**
- **1 package (32 ounces) frozen Tater Tots**
- **2 cups (16 ounces) sour cream**
- **2 cups (8 ounces) shredded cheddar cheese**

Crumble bratwurst into a large skillet; add onion. Cook over medium heat until meat is no longer pink; drain. Stir in the soup. Transfer to a greased 13-in. x 9-in. x 2-in. baking dish. Top with Tater Tots and sour cream. Sprinkle with cheese.

Bake, uncovered, at 350° for 35-40 minutes or until heated through and cheese is melted. Let stand for 5 minutes before serving. **Yield:** 6 servings.

Michigan Beans 'n' Sausage

A hot bean dish like this warms the body and the house. A simmering pot or steaming casserole of beans is always welcome.
—Elaine Schuster
Southfield, Michigan

- **1 pound dry navy beans**
- **6 bacon strips, diced**
- **3 medium onions, sliced into rings**
- **1 pound chicken gizzards, trimmed and halved, optional**
- **4 cups water**
- **2 garlic cloves, minced**
- **1 teaspoon salt**
- **1/2 teaspoon dried marjoram**
- **1 bay leaf**
- **1/8 teaspoon pepper**
- **1 pound fully cooked kielbasa *or* Polish sausage, halved lengthwise and cut into 1/4-inch slices**
- **1 can (8 ounces) tomato sauce**

1 cup soft bread crumbs
2 tablespoons butter, melted

Place beans in a Dutch oven; add water to cover by 2 in. Bring to a boil; boil for 2 minutes. Remove from the heat; cover and let stand for 1 hour. Drain and discard liquid. Return beans to pan and set aside.

In a skillet, cook bacon until crisp. Drain, reserving 2 tablespoons of drippings; set bacon aside. Saute onions and gizzards if desired in drippings until the onions are tender and the gizzards are browned. Add the 4 cups of water, garlic, salt, marjoram, bay leaf, pepper, bacon and onion mixture to the beans.

Cover and bake at 350° for 3 hours or until beans are tender. Discard bay leaf. Stir in sausage and tomato sauce. Toss bread crumbs and butter; sprinkle over top. Bake, uncovered, 25 minutes longer or until golden. **Yield:** 10-12 servings.

Pork Noodle Casserole

This is a hearty main dish. An inexpensive pork cut is tender and tasty in this savory meal-in-one casserole. —*Bernice Morris, Marshfield, Missouri*

2 cups uncooked egg noodles
2 pounds boneless pork, cut into 3/4-inch cubes
2 medium onions, chopped
2 cans (15-1/4 ounces *each*) whole kernel corn, drained
2 cans (10-3/4 ounces *each*) condensed cream of mushroom soup, undiluted
1/2 teaspoon salt
1/2 teaspoon pepper

Cook noodles according to package directions. In a large skillet, cook pork and onions over medium heat until meat is no longer pink. Drain noodles. Stir noodles, corn, soup, salt and pepper into pork mixture. Transfer to a greased 3-qt. baking dish. Cover and bake at 350° for 30 minutes. Uncover; bake 15 minutes longer. **Yield:** 8 servings.

Ham 'n' Noodle Hot Dish

(Pictured above right)

Frozen green peas add lovely color to this comforting dish. The easy, cheesy recipe is a great way to use up leftover ham. —*Renee Schwebach*
Dumont, Minnesota

3 tablespoons butter, *divided*
2 tablespoons all-purpose flour

1 cup milk
1 cup (4 ounces) shredded process American cheese
1/2 teaspoon salt
2 cups diced fully cooked ham
1-1/2 cups medium noodles, cooked and drained
1 cup frozen peas, thawed
1/4 cup dry bread crumbs
1/2 teaspoon dried parsley flakes

In a saucepan, melt 2 tablespoons butter; stir in flour until smooth. Gradually add milk. Bring to a boil over medium heat; cook and stir for 2 minutes. Remove from the heat; stir in cheese and salt until melted. Add ham, noodles and peas.

Pour into a greased 1-qt. baking dish. Melt remaining butter; add bread crumbs and parsley. Sprinkle over casserole. Bake, uncovered, at 350° for 30 minutes or until heated through. **Yield:** 4 servings.

Using Your Noodle

When preparing pasta to be used in a dish requiring further cooking—such as a casserole or soup—reduce the cooking time by a third. The pasta will continue to cook and absorb liquid in the final dish.

Franks and Corn Bread

(Pictured below)

We ate this corn bread-topped casserole often when our children were growing up, and it was always well received. It's so easy to throw together after work that I still make it for my husband and me.
—*Marilyn Hoiten, Rockford, Illinois*

2 cans (16 ounces *each*) pork and beans
1 package (12 ounces) hot dogs, halved lengthwise and sliced
2 tablespoons brown sugar
2 tablespoons Worcestershire sauce
2 tablespoons prepared mustard
1 package (8-1/2 ounces) corn bread/ muffin mix
1 cup (4 ounces) shredded cheddar cheese

In a bowl, combine the first five ingredients; mix well. Transfer to a greased 9-in. square baking dish. Prepare corn bread batter according to package directions; stir in cheese. Drop by spoonfuls onto bean mixture. Bake, uncovered, at 350° for 40-45 minutes or until heated through. **Yield:** 6 servings.

Pork Chop Casserole

(Pictured above)

One bite of these tender pork chops smothered in a creamy sauce and we could taste the care Mother put into her cooking. She was happy to share the recipe with guests who requested it after trying this delicious dish at our house. —*Nancy Duty, Jacksonville, Florida*

3/4 cup all-purpose flour
1 teaspoon salt
1/2 teaspoon pepper
6 pork chops (3/4 to 1 inch thick)
2 tablespoons vegetable oil
1 can (10-3/4 ounces) condensed cream of mushroom soup, undiluted
2/3 cup chicken broth
1/2 teaspoon ground ginger
1/4 teaspoon dried rosemary, crushed
1 cup (8 ounces) sour cream, *divided*
1 can (2.8 ounces) french-fried onions, *divided*

In a shallow bowl, combine the flour, salt and pepper; dredge pork chops. Heat oil in a large skillet; cook pork chops for 4-5 minutes per side or until browned. Place in a single layer in an ungreased 13-in. x 9-in. x 2-in. baking dish. Combine soup, broth, ginger, rosemary and 1/2 cup sour cream; pour over chops. Sprinkle with half of the onions.

Cover and bake at 350° for 45-50 minutes. Stir remaining sour cream into sauce. Top chops with remaining onions. Return to the oven, uncovered, for 10 minutes. **Yield:** 6 servings.

Creamy Spaghetti Casserole

Cottage cheese is the secret to the sauce for this hearty main dish that my family calls "Norwegian spaghetti". —*Denise Baumert, Dalhart, Texas*

1/2 cup sliced green onions
1/2 cup sliced celery
1 can (4 ounces) mushroom stems and
   pieces, drained
2 tablespoons butter
8 ounces spaghetti, cooked and drained
3 cups cubed fully cooked ham
2 cups (8 ounces) shredded Monterey
   Jack cheese, *divided*
1 cup (8 ounces) sour cream
1 cup small-curd cottage cheese
1 cup frozen cut green beans, thawed
1 jar (2 ounces) diced pimientos, drained
1/4 teaspoon garlic salt
1/8 teaspoon pepper

In a large saucepan or Dutch oven, saute onions, celery and mushrooms in butter until tender. Add the spaghetti, ham, 1-1/2 cups Monterey Jack cheese, sour cream, cottage cheese, beans, pimientos, garlic salt and pepper; mix well.

Transfer to a greased shallow 2-qt. baking dish. Bake, uncovered, at 350° for 20 minutes; sprinkle with remaining Monterey Jack cheese. Bake 10 minutes longer or until bubbly and the cheese is melted. **Yield:** 8-10 servings.

Hearty Ham Casserole

I like to fix this saucy dish when we have leftover ham. I often make it during wheat harvest. All our helpers really seem to enjoy it. —Debbie Leininger
Carpenter, Wyoming

2 cups cubed fully cooked ham
2 cups diced cooked potatoes
1 can (15-1/4 ounces) whole kernel corn,
   drained
1/4 cup minced fresh parsley
1 tablespoon chopped onion
1/4 cup butter
1/3 cup all-purpose flour
1-3/4 cups milk
1/8 teaspoon pepper
1 cup (4 ounces) shredded cheddar
   cheese *or* process American cheese

In a large bowl, combine the first four ingredients; set aside. In a saucepan, saute onion in butter for 2 minutes; stir in flour until blended. Gradually add milk and pepper. Bring to a boil; cook and stir for 2 minutes. Remove from the heat; pour over the ham mixture and stir until combined.

Transfer to a greased 11-in. x 7-in. x 2-in. baking dish. Cover and bake at 350° for 25 minutes. Uncover and sprinkle with cheese. Bake 5-10 minutes longer or until the cheese is melted. **Yield:** 4-6 servings.

Pepperoni Pizzazz

(Pictured above)

With this hearty entree, all you'll need to round out the meal is garlic bread and a tossed salad. I fix it for buffets, potluck dinners and even company.
—Marge Unger, La Porte, Indiana

8 ounces medium tube pasta
1 jar (28 ounces) spaghetti sauce, *divided*
1 jar (4-1/2 ounces) sliced mushrooms,
   drained
1 package (8 ounces) sliced pepperoni
1/2 cup chopped green pepper
1/2 cup chopped onion
1/2 cup grated Parmesan cheese
1/2 teaspoon garlic powder
1/2 teaspoon salt
1/8 teaspoon pepper
1/8 teaspoon crushed red pepper flakes
1 can (8 ounces) tomato sauce
2 cups (8 ounces) shredded mozzarella
   cheese

Cook pasta according to package directions. Meanwhile, combine 2-1/3 cups spaghetti sauce, mushrooms, pepperoni, green pepper, onion, Parmesan cheese, garlic powder, salt, pepper and red pepper flakes in a bowl. Drain pasta; add to sauce mixture and mix well.

Transfer to a greased 3-qt. baking dish. Combine the tomato sauce and remaining spaghetti sauce; pour over top. Cover and bake at 350° for 40-45 minutes or until bubbly. Sprinkle with mozzarella cheese. Bake, uncovered, 5-10 minutes longer or until cheese is melted. Let stand 5 minutes before serving. **Yield:** 9-12 servings.

Sausage Florentine Bake

(Pictured below)

Prepare once and eat twice with this delicious lasagna-like casserole! Just bake one pan and freeze the second. Later, thaw and bake it for an easy and impressive meal. The homemade sauce is so fresh-tasting. —Janice Mitchell, Aurora, Colorado

1-1/2 pounds bulk Italian sausage
    2 cans (28 ounces *each*) crushed
      tomatoes
    1 bay leaf
    3 to 4 garlic cloves, minced
    2 teaspoons sugar
    1 teaspoon dried basil
1/2 teaspoon dried oregano
1/2 teaspoon salt
1/4 teaspoon pepper
    4 eggs, beaten
1/2 cup grated Parmesan cheese, *divided*
1/8 teaspoon ground nutmeg
    2 packages (10 ounces *each*) frozen
      chopped spinach, thawed and well
      drained
    1 package (12 ounces) extra wide
      noodles, cooked and drained
    4 green onions, sliced
    4 cups (1 pound) shredded mozzarella
      cheese

In a Dutch oven, cook sausage over medium heat until no longer pink; drain. Add tomatoes, bay leaf, garlic, sugar, basil, oregano, salt and pepper; bring to a boil. Reduce heat; simmer, uncovered, for 1 hour, stirring occasionally. Meanwhile, in a bowl, combine eggs, 1/4 cup Parmesan cheese and nutmeg; mix well. Stir in spinach, noodles and onions. Discard bay leaf from sausage mixture.

In each of two greased 9-in. square baking pans, layer a fourth of the noodles and a fourth of the sausage mixture. Top each with 1 cup mozzarella cheese. Repeat layers. Top with remaining Parmesan. Bake, uncovered, at 350° for 30 minutes or until bubbly. Let stand for 10 minutes before serving. **Yield:** 2 casseroles (4 servings each).

    Editor's Note: Casseroles may be frozen before baking. Thaw in the refrigerator. Remove from refrigerator 30 minutes before baking. Bake at 350° for 1 hour.

Hawaiian Ham Bake

Take this sweet-and-sour specialty to your next potluck and get ready to hand out the recipe. When I buy a ham, I choose a large one so I'll have leftovers to use in this dish. —Judy Reist, Bloomingdale, Ontario

    3 cups cubed fully cooked ham
    1 medium onion, thinly sliced
    1 small green pepper, cut into rings
2/3 cup raisins
    1 can (8 ounces) pineapple tidbits, drained
3/4 cup packed brown sugar
    3 tablespoons cornstarch
    3 teaspoons ground mustard
1/4 teaspoon salt
1-1/2 cups pineapple juice
1/2 cup cider vinegar
4-1/2 teaspoons soy sauce
Hot cooked rice

In a greased 2-qt. baking dish, layer the ham, onion, green pepper, raisins and pineapple. In a saucepan, combine the brown sugar, cornstarch, mustard and salt. Stir in pineapple juice and vinegar until smooth. Bring to a boil; cook and stir for 2 minutes or until thickened.

    Remove from the heat; stir in soy sauce. Pour over pineapple. Cover and bake at 350° for 30 minutes or until heated through. Serve over rice. **Yield:** 4-6 servings.

Ham and Swiss Casserole

When I prepare this noodle casserole for church gatherings, it's always a hit. It can easily be doubled or tripled for a crowd. —Doris Barb, El Dorado, Kansas

1 package (8 ounces) medium noodles,
   cooked and drained
2 cups cubed fully cooked ham
2 cups (8 ounces) shredded Swiss cheese
1 can (10-3/4 ounces) condensed cream of
   celery soup, undiluted
1 cup (8 ounces) sour cream
1/2 cup chopped green pepper
1/2 cup chopped onion

In a greased 13-in. x 9-in. x 2-in. baking dish, layer
half of the noodles, ham and cheese. In a small
bowl, combine soup, sour cream, green pepper and
onion; spread half over the top. Repeat layers.
Bake, uncovered, at 350° for 40-45 minutes or until heated through. **Yield:** 6-8 servings.

Sausage Rice Casserole

*Spicy sausage provides just the right amount of zip
in this satisfying dish. It's pretty, too, with three
colors of peppers peeking through the mixture.*
—Delene Durham, Campbellsville, Kentucky

1 pound bulk hot pork sausage
1 medium onion, chopped
3 cups cooked rice
1 *each* medium green, sweet red and
   yellow pepper, diced
1 can (10-3/4 ounces) condensed cream of
   mushroom soup, undiluted
1 can (10-1/2 ounces) condensed French
   onion soup, undiluted

In a large skillet over medium heat, cook sausage
and onion until sausage is no longer pink and onion
is tender; drain. Add the rice, peppers and soups;
mix well. Transfer to an ungreased 13-in. x 9-in. x
2-in. baking dish. Bake, uncovered, at 350° for
30-35 minutes or until bubbly. **Yield:** 6-8 servings.

Corn Dog Casserole

(Pictured above right)

*Reminiscent of traditional corn dogs, this fun main
dish really hits the spot on fall days. It's perfect for
the football parties my husband and I often host.
It tastes especially good right from the oven.*
—Marcy Suzanne Olipane, Belleville, Illinois

2 cups thinly sliced celery
2 tablespoons butter
1-1/2 cups sliced green onions
1-1/2 pounds hot dogs
2 eggs

1-1/2 cups milk
2 teaspoons rubbed sage
1/4 teaspoon pepper
2 packages (8-1/2 ounces *each*) corn
   bread/muffin mix
2 cups (8 ounces) shredded sharp
   cheddar cheese, *divided*

In a skillet, saute celery in butter for 5 minutes. Add
onions; saute for 5 minutes. Place in a large bowl;
set aside. Cut hot dogs lengthwise into quarters,
then cut into thirds. In the same skillet, saute the hot
dogs for 5 minutes or until lightly browned; add to
vegetables. Set aside 1 cup.

In a large bowl, combine eggs, milk, sage and
pepper. Add the remaining hot dog mixture. Stir in
corn bread mixes. Add 1-1/2 cups of cheese.
Spread into a shallow 3-qt. baking dish. Top with reserved hot dog mixture and remaining cheese.
Bake, uncovered, at 400° for 30 minutes or until
golden brown. **Yield:** 12 servings.

Ham Hints

Choose firm, plump ham that is rosy pink
and finely grained. When using ham as a
flavoring in soups, casseroles, bean dishes
or stir-fries, finely chop the meat. You'll get
more intense, evenly distributed flavor than
with a few large chunks.

chops with syrup; sprinkle with the salt and remaining cinnamon. Bake, uncovered, for 5-10 minutes or until meat juices run clear. **Yield:** 4 servings.

Pepperoni Potatoes

On lazy Saturdays, my family really enjoys this comforting casserole. I rely on convenient O'Brien potatoes, bits of pepperoni, mozzarella cheese and sweet red pepper for the hearty dish.
—*Brenda Schrag*
Farmington, New Mexico

> 3 tablespoons butter
> 2 tablespoons all-purpose flour
> 2 cups milk
> 1 teaspoon salt
> 1/2 teaspoon dried thyme
> 1/2 teaspoon dried parsley flakes
> 1/4 teaspoon dried basil
> 1/8 teaspoon pepper
> 1 package (28 ounces) frozen O'Brien
>   hash brown potatoes, thawed
> 1/4 cup chopped sweet red pepper
> 1 cup frozen corn, thawed
> 1 cup (4 ounces) shredded mozzarella
>   cheese
> 27 slices pepperoni, quartered

In a small saucepan, melt the butter over medium heat. Stir in flour until smooth. Gradually stir in milk. Bring to a boil; cook and stir for 2 minutes or until thickened. Remove from the heat. Stir in the seasonings.

In a greased 13-in. x 9-in. x 2-in. baking dish, layer the potatoes, red pepper and corn. Top with the white sauce, cheese and pepperoni. Bake, uncovered, at 375° for 25-30 minutes or until heated through. **Yield:** 12-15 servings.

Bean and Pork Chop Bake

(Pictured above)

Having grown up on a pork-producing farm, I like to include that versatile meat in many recipes. This one, featuring pork chops, has an apple-cinnamon flavor with a hint of sweet maple. It's particularly good when fall apples are in season.
—*LaRita Lang, Lincoln, Nebraska*

> 4 boneless pork loin chops
>   (1/2 inch thick)
> 1 tablespoon vegetable oil
> 1 large tart apple, peeled and chopped
> 1 small onion, chopped
> 1 can (28 ounces) baked beans
> 1/3 cup raisins
> 1/4 teaspoon ground cinnamon, *divided*
> 1 tablespoon maple pancake syrup
> 1/4 teaspoon salt

In a large skillet, brown pork chops on both sides in oil. Remove and keep warm. In same pan, saute apple and onion until tender. Stir in beans, raisins and 1/8 teaspoon cinnamon. Spoon into a greased 2-1/2-qt. baking dish; top with pork chops.
Cover and bake at 350° for 40 minutes. Brush

Sparerib Casserole

This is an old Southern recipe my mother passed on to me many, many years ago. It's especially good for a Saturday night supper.
—*Doris Voytovich*
Inkster, Michigan

> 4 to 5 pounds pork spareribs, cut into
>   individual ribs
> 2 teaspoons salt, *divided*
> 1/2 teaspoon pepper, *divided*
> 5 tablespoons vegetable oil, *divided*
> 6 cups cubed potatoes
> 1 medium onion, sliced
> 2 garlic cloves, minced

4 teaspoons all-purpose flour
2 tablespoons dried parsley flakes
1 can (12 ounces) evaporated milk
1/8 teaspoon paprika

Sprinkle ribs with 1 teaspoon salt and 1/4 teaspoon pepper. In a large skillet, brown ribs in 3 tablespoons oil in batches. Place ribs on a rack in a shallow roasting pan. Bake, uncovered, at 350° for 20 minutes. Turn the ribs and bake 20 minutes longer. Pat dry.

Place potatoes in a saucepan and cover with water; cover and bring to a boil over medium-high heat. Cook for 15-20 minutes or until tender. Meanwhile, in a saucepan, saute onion and garlic in remaining oil until tender. Stir in the flour, parsley, and remaining salt and pepper until blended. Gradually stir in milk. Bring to a boil; cook and stir for 2 minutes or until thickened.

Drain potatoes; place in a greased 13-in. x 9-in. x 2-in. baking dish. Top with sauce and ribs. Cover and bake at 350° for 15 minutes. Uncover; sprinkle with paprika. Bake 5-10 minutes longer or until ribs are tender and potatoes are heated through. **Yield:** 6 servings.

Jambalaya Casserole

(Pictured below right)

Whenever family and friends get together, this is the dish I am asked to prepare. It's delicious, economical and easy to fix. —Evelynn Anderson Lugo
Kenner, Louisiana

 3 large onions, chopped
 3 large green peppers, chopped
 3 celery ribs, chopped
 12 garlic cloves, minced
 1-1/2 cups butter
 3 pounds fully cooked smoked sausage, cut into 1/2-inch slices
 9 cups chicken broth
 6 cups uncooked long grain rice
 3 cups chopped fresh tomatoes
 1-1/2 cups chopped green onions
 1/2 cup minced fresh parsley
 3 tablespoons Worcestershire sauce
 3 tablespoons hot pepper sauce
 3 tablespoons browning sauce, optional
 1 tablespoon salt
 1 tablespoon pepper

In a large skillet, saute onions, green peppers, celery and garlic in butter until crisp-tender. Place in a very large bowl; stir in remaining ingredients.

Transfer to three greased shallow 3-qt. baking dishes. Cover and bake at 375° for 45-50 minutes or until rice is tender, stirring twice. **Yield:** 3 casseroles (8 servings each).

Pasta Ham Hot Dish

I brought this simple casserole to a potluck at work and it was a hit. You can use a pound of browned ground beef in place of the ham. —Judie Porath
Summit, South Dakota

 4 ounces uncooked spaghetti, broken into 2-inch pieces
 1/4 cup chopped onion
 1 tablespoon butter
 2 cups cubed fully cooked ham
 1 can (15-1/4 ounces) whole kernel corn, drained
 1 can (14-3/4 ounces) cream-style corn
 1 cup cubed process cheese (Velveeta)
 1/2 teaspoon seasoned salt

Cook spaghetti according to package directions. Meanwhile, in a small skillet, saute onion in butter until tender. Drain spaghetti; place in a large bowl.

Add the ham, corn, cheese, seasoned salt and onion mixture. Transfer to a greased 2-qt. baking dish. Cover and bake at 350° for 30-35 minutes or until the cheese is melted, stirring once. **Yield:** 4-6 servings.

Seafood

Microwave Tuna Casserole, p. 70

Chapter 5

Special Shrimp Bake

(Pictured below)

My husband and I entertain most weekends, and to me the easiest way of serving a crowd is a buffet. This dish, a change of pace from turkey during the holidays, can be put together the night before, then baked the following day. —Kathy Houchen
Waldorf, Maryland

> 3 quarts water
> 1 tablespoon plus 1 teaspoon salt, *divided*
> 2-1/2 pounds uncooked medium shrimp, peeled and deveined
> 2 tablespoons vegetable oil
> 1 tablespoon lemon juice
> 1/4 cup finely chopped green pepper
> 1/4 cup finely chopped onion
> 2 tablespoons butter
> 1 can (10-3/4 ounces) condensed tomato soup, undiluted
> 1 cup heavy whipping cream
> 2-1/4 cups cooked rice
> 1/8 teaspoon *each* ground mace, pepper and cayenne pepper
> 1/2 cup slivered almonds, toasted, *divided*

In a Dutch oven, bring water and 1 tablespoon salt to a boil. Add shrimp; cook for 3 minutes or until pink. Drain. Sprinkle shrimp with oil and lemon juice; set aside. In a skillet, saute green pepper and onion in butter for 5 minutes or until tender. Add soup, cream, rice, mace, pepper, cayenne, 1/4 cup of almonds and remaining salt. Set aside 1 cup of shrimp. Add remaining shrimp to the rice mixture.

Transfer to a greased 2-qt. baking dish. Bake, uncovered, at 350° for 30-35 minutes. Top with reserved shrimp and remaining almonds; bake 20 minutes longer or until the shrimp are lightly browned. **Yield:** 8-10 servings.

Spinach Tuna Casserole

After a busy day of bookkeeping for our family contracting business, I count on this rapid recipe my mother passed along to me. I double it if I need to feed unexpected guests who stop by at mealtime.
—Nancy Adams, Hancock, New Hampshire

> 1 package (10 ounces) frozen chopped spinach, thawed and squeezed dry
> 1 can (6 ounces) tuna, drained
> 1/3 cup seasoned bread crumbs
> 3 tablespoons crushed seasoned stuffing
> 1/4 teaspoon salt
> 1/2 cup mayonnaise
> 1/4 cup sour cream
> 2 to 3 teaspoons lemon juice
> 2 to 3 tablespoons Parmesan cheese

In a bowl, combine the first five ingredients; mix well. Combine the mayonnaise, sour cream and lemon juice; add to tuna mixture and mix well.

Transfer to a greased 2-cup baking dish. Sprinkle with Parmesan cheese. Cover and bake at 350° for 20-25 minutes or until heated through. **Yield:** 2 servings.

Editor's Note: Reduced-fat or fat-free mayonnaise is not recommended for this recipe.

Favorite Halibut Casserole

I've been using this recipe since my college days. I even took it to Western Samoa when I was teaching school there. You can substitute any whitefish for the halibut. —Gayle Brown, Millville, Utah

> 5 tablespoons butter, *divided*
> 1/4 cup all-purpose flour
> 1/2 teaspoon salt
> 1/8 to 1/4 teaspoon white pepper
> 1-1/2 cups milk
> 1 small green pepper, chopped
> 1 small onion, chopped

        2 cups cubed cooked halibut (about 1
            pound)
        3 hard-cooked eggs, chopped
        1 jar (2 ounces) diced pimientos, drained
    1/3 cup shredded cheddar cheese

In a large saucepan, melt 4 tablespoons butter. Stir in flour, salt and pepper until smooth. Gradually add milk. Bring to a boil; cook and stir for 2 minutes or until thickened. Remove from the heat; cover and set aside. In a small skillet, saute green pepper and onion in remaining butter until tender. Stir into white sauce. Add the halibut, eggs and pimientos.

Transfer to a greased 1-1/2-qt. baking dish. Sprinkle with cheese. Bake, uncovered, at 375° for 15-20 minutes or until bubbly. **Yield:** 4 servings.

Blend of the Bayou

My sister-in-law shared this recipe when I first moved to Louisiana. It's been handed down in my husband's family for generations. It's quick to prepare, nutritious and beautiful. —*Ruby Williams Bogalusa, Louisiana*

    1 package (8 ounces) cream cheese,
        cubed
    4 tablespoons butter, *divided*
    1 large onion, chopped
    2 celery ribs, chopped
    1 large green pepper, chopped
    1 pound cooked medium shrimp, peeled
        and deveined
    2 cans (6 ounces *each*) crabmeat, drained,
        flaked and cartilage removed
    1 can (10-3/4 ounces) condensed cream of
        mushroom soup, undiluted
    1 jar (4-1/2 ounces) sliced mushrooms,
        drained
    1 teaspoon garlic salt
    3/4 teaspoon hot pepper sauce
    1/2 teaspoon cayenne pepper
    3/4 cup cooked rice
    3/4 cup shredded cheddar cheese
    1/2 cup crushed butter-flavored crackers
        (about 12 crackers)

In a small saucepan, cook and stir the cream cheese and 2 tablespoons butter over low heat until melted and smooth. In a large skillet, saute the onion, celery and green pepper in remaining butter until tender; stir in cream cheese mixture. Stir in the shrimp, crab, soup, mushrooms, garlic salt, hot pepper sauce, cayenne and rice.

Transfer to a greased 2-qt. baking dish. Combine cheese and cracker crumbs; sprinkle over the top. Bake, uncovered, at 350° for 25-30 minutes or until bubbly. **Yield:** 6-8 servings.

Crab Supreme

(Pictured above)

I came across this recipe years ago in an old church cookbook. It's so good, I've even served it for Christmas dinner. —*Cheryl Ryan, Timberville, Virginia*

    1 small onion, finely chopped
    1/4 cup diced green pepper
    3 tablespoons butter, *divided*
    1 tablespoon all-purpose flour
    3/4 cup milk
    1/2 teaspoon chili powder
    1/4 teaspoon salt
    1/2 pound fresh *or* canned crabmeat,
        drained, flaked and cartilage removed
        or 1 cup imitation crab meat, flaked
    1/3 cup mayonnaise
Dash hot pepper sauce
    2 tablespoons dry bread crumbs
Dash paprika

In a small saucepan, saute onion and green pepper in 2 tablespoons butter. Stir in flour until blended; gradually stir in the milk. Add chili powder and salt. Bring to a boil; cook and stir for 1 minute or until thickened. Remove from the heat; stir in the crab, mayonnaise and hot pepper sauce.

Transfer to a greased shallow 1-qt. baking dish. Melt the remaining butter and toss with bread crumbs. Sprinkle over the crab mixture. Bake, uncovered, at 350° for 25-30 minutes or until heated through. Sprinkle with paprika before serving. **Yield:** 2-3 servings.

Editor's Note: Reduced-fat or fat-free mayonnaise is not recommended for this recipe.

greased 13-in. x 9-in. x 2-in. baking dish.

For dough, combine biscuit mix and milk until blended. On a lightly floured surface, roll dough into a 12-in. x 9-in. rectangle. Sprinkle with cheese, pimientos and parsley. Roll up jelly-roll style starting with a long side. Cut into 1-in. slices; place over tuna mixture. Beat egg and water; brush over swirls. Bake, uncovered, at 400° for 20-25 minutes or until top is lightly browned. **Yield:** 6-8 servings.

Pasta Crab Casserole

(Pictured below)

This is an easy dish to freeze ahead for company. A yummy combination of spiral pasta, crab and sauteed veggies is coated with a buttery sauce, then covered with cheddar cheese. All that's needed to complete the meal is a tossed green salad.
— *Georgia Mountain, Tampa, Florida*

    8 ounces uncooked spiral pasta
    2 large onions, chopped
1/2 pound fresh mushrooms, sliced
1/2 cup chopped green pepper
    2 garlic cloves, minced
1/2 cup butter
    2 packages (8 ounces *each*) imitation
        crabmeat, chopped
1/2 cup sour cream

Tuna Bake with Cheese Swirls

(Pictured above)

My family thinks this dish is a tasty alternative to regular tuna casserole. The proof is that there are never any leftovers.
— *Virginia Magee Reene, New Hampshire*

    3 tablespoons chopped onion
    3 tablespoons chopped green pepper
1/3 cup butter
1/3 cup all-purpose flour
    3 cups milk
    1 can (10-3/4 ounces) condensed cream of
        mushroom soup, undiluted
    1 can (12 ounces) tuna, drained and flaked
    1 tablespoon lemon juice
    1 teaspoon salt
DOUGH:
    2 cups biscuit/baking mix
1/2 cup milk
1/2 cup shredded cheddar cheese
1/2 cup diced pimientos
1/4 cup minced fresh parsley
    1 egg
    2 teaspoons water

In a saucepan, saute onion and green pepper in butter. Blend in the flour until smooth. Gradually stir in milk; bring to a boil over medium heat. Cook and stir for 2 minutes. Remove from the heat; stir in soup, tuna, lemon juice and salt. Pour into an un-

        2 teaspoons salt
1-1/2 teaspoons dried basil
1-1/2 cups (6 ounces) shredded cheddar
        cheese

Cook pasta according to package directions. Meanwhile, in a skillet, saute onions, mushrooms, green pepper and garlic in butter until crisp-tender. Remove from heat. Drain pasta; add to vegetable mixture. Stir in crab, sour cream, salt and basil.

Transfer to two greased 8-in. square baking dishes. Sprinkle with cheese. Cover and freeze one casserole for up to 1 month. Cover and bake the second casserole at 350° for 20 minutes. Uncover and bake 5 minutes longer.

To use frozen casserole: Thaw in the refrigerator for 24 hours. Remove from the refrigerator 30 minutes before baking. Cover and bake at 350° for 55-60 minutes or until heated through. **Yield:** 2 casseroles (4-6 servings each).

Salmon Stroganoff

A golden bread crumb topping is the finishing touch on this rich noodle casserole that takes advantage of canned salmon from the pantry. It's so good that I'm always asked for the recipe.
—*Joan Sherlock, Belle Plaine, Minnesota*

    4 cups cooked wide egg noodles
    1 can (14-3/4 ounces) salmon, drained,
        bones and skin removed
    1 jar (4-1/2 ounces) sliced mushrooms,
        drained
    1 jar (2 ounces) diced pimientos, drained
1-1/2 cups small-curd cottage cheese
1-1/2 cups (12 ounces) sour cream
    1/2 cup mayonnaise
    3 tablespoons grated onion
    1 garlic clove, minced
1-1/2 teaspoons Worcestershire sauce
    1 teaspoon salt
    1 cup (4 ounces) shredded cheddar
        cheese
    1/3 cup dry bread crumbs
    2 tablespoons butter, melted

In a bowl, combine the noodles, salmon, mushrooms and pimientos. Combine cottage cheese, sour cream, mayonnaise, onion, garlic, Worcestershire sauce and salt; add to noodle mixture and mix well. Stir in cheddar cheese.

Transfer to a greased 2-qt. baking dish. Toss bread crumbs and butter; sprinkle over the casserole. Bake, uncovered, at 350° for 30-35 minutes or until bubbly. **Yield:** 4-6 servings.

Editor's Note: Reduced-fat or fat-free mayonnaise is not recommended for this recipe.

Catch-of-the-Day Casserole

(Pictured above)

This super salmon recipe comes from my dear mother-in-law. She's one of the best cooks and one of the best mothers I know. —*Cathy Clugston*
Cloverdale, Indiana

    4 ounces small shell pasta
    1 can (10-3/4 ounces) condensed cream of
        celery soup, undiluted
    1/2 cup mayonnaise
    1/4 cup milk
    1/4 cup shredded cheddar cheese
    1 package (10 ounces) frozen peas,
        thawed
    1 can (7-1/2 ounces) salmon, drained,
        bones and skin removed
    1 tablespoon finely chopped onion

Cook pasta according to package directions. Meanwhile, in a bowl, combine the soup, mayonnaise, milk and cheese until blended. Stir in peas, salmon and onion. Drain pasta; add to salmon mixture. Transfer to a greased 2-qt. baking dish. Bake, uncovered, at 350° for 30-35 minutes or until bubbly. **Yield:** 4 servings.

Editor's Note: Reduced-fat or fat-free mayonnaise is not recommended for this recipe.

Fish Stick Supper

(Pictured below)

Dill adds fresh flavor to this comforting combination of foods you likely keep in your freezer. When our children were growing up, they loved this meal. It's a unique way to serve fish sticks.
—*Ruth Andrewson, Leavenworth, Washington*

    1 package (12 ounces) frozen shredded
      hash brown potatoes, thawed
    4 eggs
    2 cups milk
    1 tablespoon dried minced onion
    1 tablespoon snipped fresh dill *or* 1
      teaspoon dill weed
1-1/4 teaspoons seasoned salt
  1/8 teaspoon pepper
    1 cup (4 ounces) shredded cheddar
      cheese
    1 package (12 ounces) frozen fish sticks
      (about 18 fish sticks)

Break apart hash browns with a fork; set aside. In a large bowl, beat eggs and milk. Add onion, dill, seasoned salt and pepper. Stir in hash browns and cheese. Transfer to a greased 11-in. x 7-in. x 2-in. baking dish; arrange fish sticks over the top. Bake, uncovered, at 350° for 50 minutes or until top is golden brown and fish flakes with a fork. Let stand for 5 minutes before cutting. **Yield:** 6 servings.

Asparagus Crab Au Gratin

I was delighted to discover this rich casserole years ago when we had a large asparagus patch. It's so easy that I've fixed it many times since.
—*Nancy Thibodeau, Overgaard, Arizona*

    1 package (10 ounces) frozen asparagus
      cuts, thawed and drained
    1 can (6 ounces) crabmeat, drained, flaked
      and cartilage removed *or* 1 cup flaked
      imitation crabmeat
  1/2 cup shredded cheddar cheese
    4 tablespoons butter, *divided*
    2 tablespoons all-purpose flour
    1 cup milk
  1/2 teaspoon ground mustard
  1/2 teaspoon salt
  1/8 teaspoon pepper
    2 teaspoons lemon juice
    1 cup soft bread crumbs

Place asparagus in a greased 1-qt. baking dish. Top with crab and sprinkle with cheese; set aside. In a saucepan, melt 2 tablespoons butter. Stir in flour until smooth. Whisk in milk, mustard, salt and pepper. Bring to a boil over medium heat; cook and stir for 2 minutes or until thickened.

Remove from the heat; stir in lemon juice. Pour over asparagus. Melt remaining butter; toss with bread crumbs. Sprinkle over top. Bake, uncovered, at 350° for 30 minutes or until heated through. **Yield:** 4 servings.

Microwave Tuna Casserole

(Pictured on page 64)

My family digs into this moist, flavorful tuna casserole. Crisp celery along with zucchini and tomato give it a fresh twist. When I get home from work and we have to be somewhere else in 90 minutes, this is the recipe I rely on. —*Laura Montoya*
Williams Lake, British Columbia

  1/2 cup sour cream
  1/2 cup mayonnaise
    2 teaspoons prepared mustard
  1/2 teaspoon salt
  1/2 teaspoon dried thyme
  1/4 teaspoon dill weed
    5 cups cooked egg noodles

2 cans (6 ounces *each*) tuna, drained and
  flaked
1/2 cup chopped celery
1/3 cup sliced green onions
1 small zucchini, sliced
1 cup (4 ounces) shredded cheddar
  cheese
1 medium tomato, chopped

In a small bowl, combine the first six ingredients;
mix well. In a large bowl, combine noodles, tuna,
celery and onions. Stir in the sour cream mixture.
Spoon half into a greased 2-qt. microwave-safe
dish; top with half of the zucchini. Repeat layers.

Microwave, uncovered, on high for 6-8 minutes
or until heated through. Sprinkle with cheese and
tomato. Microwave, uncovered, 2 minutes longer.
Let stand for 3 minutes before serving. **Yield:** 6
servings.

Editor's Note: Reduced-fat or fat-free mayonnaise is not recommended for this recipe. This
recipe was tested in an 850-watt microwave.

Swiss Tuna Bake

*My husband enjoys cooking just as much as I do.
One night he tossed together this comforting casserole from meager ingredients we had in our cup-
board. It turned out to be the best-tasting tuna
casserole I have ever had!* —*Joanne Callahan
Far Hills, New Jersey*

4 cups cooked medium egg noodles
1-1/2 cups (6 ounces) shredded Swiss cheese
1 cup mayonnaise
1 can (6 ounces) tuna, drained and flaked
1 cup seasoned bread crumbs, *divided*

In a large bowl, combine the noodles, cheese, mayonnaise and tuna. Sprinkle 1/2 cup bread crumbs
into a greased 9-in. square baking dish. Spread noodle mixture over crumbs. Sprinkle with the remaining crumbs. Bake, uncovered, at 350° for 20 minutes
or until heated through. **Yield:** 4 servings.

Editor's Note: Reduced-fat or fat-free mayonnaise is not recommended for this recipe.

Cheddar Shrimp And Penne

(Pictured above right)

*My wife and I take turns in the kitchen. When I
created this creamy dish, it quickly became one of
our favorites.* —*Brad Walker, Holt, Michigan*

2 cups uncooked penne *or* other medium
  tube pasta
2 garlic cloves, minced
2 tablespoons butter
2 tablespoons all-purpose flour
1/2 teaspoon salt
1/4 teaspoon pepper
2 cups milk
1-1/2 cups (6 ounces) shredded cheddar
  cheese, *divided*
1 pound cooked medium shrimp, peeled
  and deveined
1 can (15-1/4 ounces) whole kernel corn,
  drained

Cook pasta according to package directions. Meanwhile, in a large saucepan, cook the garlic in
butter over medium heat for 1 minute. Stir in flour,
salt and pepper until blended. Gradually add milk.
Bring to a boil; cook and stir for 2 minutes or until
thickened. Reduce heat; stir in 1 cup of cheese
until melted. Remove from the heat.

Drain pasta; add pasta, shrimp and corn to
cheese sauce. Transfer to a greased 2-qt. baking
dish. Cover and bake at 350° for 25 minutes. Uncover; sprinkle with remaining cheese. Bake 10-15 minutes longer or until bubbly. **Yield:** 4-6 servings.

Something Fishy

Remove the fishy smell from your hands,
knife and cutting board by rubbing them
thoroughly with lemon wedges.

Pour into a greased 2-qt. baking dish. Cover and bake at 350° for 25-30 minutes or until bubbly. **Yield:** 4-6 servings.

Golden Tuna Casserole

(Pictured above)

Mushrooms, green pepper and onion are added to boxed macaroni and cheese in this comforting take on the classic tuna bake. It is a delicious, hearty and quick-to-fix dinner. I serve it with a tossed salad and hot rolls. —Helen Suter, Golconda, Illinois

- 1 package (7-1/4 ounces) macaroni and cheese mix
- 1/2 cup chopped onion
- 1/4 cup chopped green pepper
- 1/3 cup butter
- 3/4 cup milk
- 1 can (10-3/4 ounces) condensed cream of celery soup, undiluted
- 1 can (6 ounces) tuna, drained
- 1 jar (4-1/2 ounces) sliced mushrooms, drained
- 1 jar (2 ounces) diced pimientos, drained

Set aside the cheese sauce packet. In a saucepan, cook macaroni according to package directions; drain and set aside. In the same pan, saute onion and green pepper in butter. Return macaroni to the pan. Add milk and contents of cheese sauce packet; stir until smooth. Stir in the soup, tuna, mushrooms and pimientos.

Lobster Newburg

(Pictured below)

We live in Maine, so we like to use fresh lobster in this time-honored recipe. However, it can also be made with frozen, canned or imitation lobster. No matter how you prepare it, guests will think you fussed when you serve these individual casseroles. —Wendy Cornell, Hudson, Maine

- 3 cups fresh, frozen *or* canned flaked lobster meat *or* imitation lobster chunks
- 3 tablespoons butter
- 1/4 teaspoon paprika
- 3 cups heavy whipping cream
- 1/2 teaspoon Worcestershire sauce
- 3 egg yolks, lightly beaten
- 1 tablespoon sherry *or* water
- 1/4 teaspoon salt
- 1/3 cup crushed butter-flavored crackers (about 8 crackers)

In a large skillet, saute the lobster in butter and paprika for 3-4 minutes; set aside. In a large saucepan, bring cream and Worcestershire sauce to a gentle boil. Meanwhile, in a bowl, combine egg yolks, sherry or water and salt.

Remove cream from the heat; stir a small amount into egg yolk mixture. Return all to the pan, stirring constantly. Bring to a gentle boil; cook and

stir for 5-7 minutes or until slightly thickened. Stir in the lobster.

Divide lobster mixture between four 10-oz. individual baking dishes. Sprinkle with cracker crumbs. Broil 6 in. from the heat for 2-3 minutes or until golden brown. **Yield:** 4 servings.

Salmon Macaroni Bake

A neighbor brought us this creamy casserole the night after our newborn daughter came home from the hospital. —Carrie Mitchell
Raleigh, North Carolina

  1 package (14 ounces) deluxe macaroni
    and cheese dinner mix
  1 can (10-3/4 ounces) condensed cream of
    mushroom soup, undiluted
1/2 cup milk
  1 can (6 ounces) skinless boneless
    salmon, drained
  1 tablespoon grated onion *or* 1/2
    teaspoon onion powder
1/2 cup shredded cheddar cheese
1/2 cup dry bread crumbs
  2 tablespoons butter, cubed

Prepare macaroni and cheese according to package directions. Stir in the soup, milk, salmon, onion and cheddar cheese. Transfer to a greased 1-1/2-qt. baking dish. Sprinkle with bread crumbs; dot with butter. Bake, uncovered, at 375° for 30 minutes or until heated through. **Yield:** 4 servings.

Oven Jambalaya

If you're looking for an easy but delicious version of jambalaya, this is it. —Ruby Williams
Bogalusa, Louisiana

2-1/4 cups water
1-1/2 cups uncooked long grain rice
  1 can (10-3/4 ounces) condensed cream of
    celery soup, undiluted
  1 can (10-3/4 ounces) condensed cream of
    onion soup, undiluted
  1 can (10 ounces) diced tomatoes and
    green chilies, undrained
  1 pound fully cooked smoked sausage,
    cut into 1/2-inch slices
  1 pound cooked medium shrimp, peeled
    and deveined

In a large bowl, combine the first five ingredients; mix well. Pour into a greased 13-in. x 9-in. x 2-in. baking dish. Cover and bake at 350° for 40 minutes.

Stir in sausage and shrimp. Cover and bake 20-30 minutes longer or until the rice is tender. **Yield:** 8-10 servings.

Baked Fish and Rice

(Pictured above)

Fish and rice are a tasty change of pace from traditional meat-and-potato fare. —Jo Groth
Plainfield, Iowa

1-1/2 cups boiling chicken broth
  1/2 cup uncooked long grain rice
  1/4 teaspoon Italian seasoning
  1/4 teaspoon garlic powder
    1 package (10 ounces) frozen chopped
      broccoli, thawed and drained
    1 tablespoon grated Parmesan cheese
    1 can (2.8 ounces) french-fried onions,
      divided
    1 pound fresh *or* frozen fish fillets, thawed
Dash paprika
  1/2 cup shredded cheddar cheese

In a greased 11-in. x 7-in. x 2-in. baking dish, combine the broth, rice, Italian seasoning and garlic powder. Cover and bake at 375° for 10 minutes. Add broccoli, Parmesan cheese and half of onions. Top with fish fillets; sprinkle with paprika.

Cover and bake 20-25 minutes longer or until the fish flakes easily with a fork. Uncover; sprinkle with cheddar cheese and remaining onions. Return to the oven for 3 minutes or until cheese is melted. **Yield:** 4 servings.

New England Fish Bake

(Pictured below)

This is one of my favorite seafood dishes. My mother-in-law gave me the recipe.
—*Norma DesRoches, Warwick, Rhode Island*

> 4 medium potatoes, peeled
> 1 teaspoon all-purpose flour
> 1 small onion, sliced and separated
>   into rings
> 1/2 teaspoon salt
> 1/4 teaspoon pepper
> 3/4 cup milk, *divided*
> 1-1/2 pounds cod, trout, catfish *or* pike fillets
> 3 tablespoons grated Parmesan cheese,
>   optional
> 2 tablespoons minced fresh parsley
> 1/4 teaspoon paprika

Place potatoes in a saucepan and cover with water; cover and bring to a boil over medium-high heat. Cook for 15-20 minutes or until almost tender; drain. Cut into 1/8-in.-thick slices; place in a greased shallow 2-qt. baking dish. Sprinkle with flour. Top with onion; sprinkle with salt and pepper.

Pour half of the milk over potatoes. Top with fish and remaining milk. Sprinkle with Parmesan cheese if desired. Cover and bake at 375° for 20-30 minutes or until fish flakes easily with a fork. Sprinkle with parsley and paprika before serving. **Yield:** 3-4 servings.

Angel Hair Shrimp Bake

Shrimp and pasta blend beautifully with the herbs, salsa and three kinds of cheese in this hearty layered casserole. The shrimp make this dish special enough for guests, but your family is sure to enjoy it, too. —*Susan Davidson, Elm Grove, Wisconsin*

✓ Uses less fat, sugar or salt. Includes Nutritional Analysis and Diabetic Exchanges.

> 1 package (9 ounces) refrigerated angel
>   hair pasta
> 1-1/2 pounds uncooked medium shrimp,
>   peeled and deveined
> 3/4 cup crumbled feta cheese
> 1/2 cup shredded Swiss cheese
> 1 jar (16 ounces) chunky salsa
> 1/2 cup shredded Monterey Jack cheese
> 3/4 cup minced fresh parsley
> 1 teaspoon dried basil
> 1 teaspoon dried oregano
> 2 eggs
> 1 cup half-and-half cream
> 1 cup (8 ounces) plain yogurt

In a greased 13-in. x 9-in. x 2-in. baking dish, layer half of the pasta, shrimp, feta cheese, Swiss cheese and salsa. Repeat layers. Sprinkle with Monterey Jack cheese, parsley, basil and oregano.

In a small bowl, whisk eggs, cream and yogurt; pour over casserole. Bake, uncovered, at 350° for 25-30 minutes or until shrimp turn pink and pasta is tender. Let stand for 5 minutes before serving. **Yield:** 12 servings.

Nutritional Analysis: 1 serving (prepared with reduced-fat Swiss and Monterey Jack cheeses and fat-free half-and-half) equals 230 calories, 6 g fat (3 g saturated fat), 135 mg cholesterol, 556 mg sodium, 23 g carbohydrate, 1 g fiber, 22 g protein. **Diabetic Exchanges:** 2-1/2 lean meat, 1-1/2 starch.

Crab Rockefeller

When you're entertaining seafood lovers, you can't go wrong with this delightful main course. It has such rich flavor! The spinach and golden crumb topping make the casserole look very attractive.
—*Cheryl Maczko, Arthurdale, West Virginia*

4 tablespoons butter, *divided*
2 tablespoons all-purpose flour
1-1/3 cups milk
1/2 cup grated Parmesan cheese
1 package (10 ounces) frozen chopped
    spinach, thawed and squeezed dry
1 can (6 ounces) crabmeat, drained, flaked
    and cartilage removed
1/2 cup dry bread crumbs

In a saucepan, melt 2 tablespoons butter. Stir in flour until smooth; gradually add the milk. Bring to a boil; cook and stir for 2 minutes or until thickened. Reduce heat; stir in the cheese until smooth. Add the spinach and crab.

Transfer to a greased shallow 1-qt. baking dish. Melt the remaining butter and toss with the bread crumbs. Sprinkle over the top. Bake, uncovered, at 375° for 15-20 minutes or until bubbly. **Yield:** 3-4 servings.

Pecan Salmon Casserole

Peas, pecans and pimientos complement the salmon in this potluck-perfect dish that's topped with crushed potato chips that give it added crunch. It's great for family dinners, too.   —Edna Coburn
Tucson, Arizona

1 package (16 ounces) small shell pasta
2 medium onions, finely chopped
1/2 pound sliced fresh mushrooms
1/4 cup butter, cubed
2 cans (10-3/4 ounces *each*) condensed
    cream of mushroom soup, undiluted
1-1/2 cups milk
2 teaspoons Worcestershire sauce
1 teaspoon salt
1/2 teaspoon pepper
2 cans (14-3/4 ounces *each*) salmon,
    drained, bones and skin removed
2 cups frozen peas
1 cup chopped pecans, toasted
1 jar (2 ounces) diced pimientos,
    drained
1/2 cup crushed potato chips

Cook pasta according to package directions. Meanwhile, in a large skillet, saute the onions and mushrooms in butter until tender. Stir in the soup, milk, Worcestershire sauce, salt and pepper until blended; bring to a boil. Remove from the heat.

Drain pasta. Add the pasta, salmon, peas, pecans and pimientos to the skillet. Transfer to a greased shallow 3-qt. baking dish. Cover and bake at 350° for 30-35 minutes or until heated through. Sprinkle with potato chips. **Yield:** 12 servings.

Tuna in the Straw Casserole

(Pictured above)

Shoestring potatoes give this main dish great flavor and crunch. Even my husband, who doesn't normally care for tuna, counts it among his favorites.
—Kallee McCreery, Escondido, California

1 can (10-3/4 ounces) condensed cream of
    mushroom soup, undiluted
1 can (5 ounces) evaporated milk
1 can (6 ounces) tuna, drained and flaked
1 can (4 ounces) mushroom stems and
    pieces, drained
1 cup frozen mixed vegetables, thawed
2 cups potato sticks, *divided*

In a bowl, combine the soup and milk until blended. Stir in the tuna, mushrooms, vegetables and 1-1/2 cups potato sticks.

Transfer to a greased 1-1/2-qt. baking dish. Bake, uncovered, at 375° for 20 minutes. Sprinkle with the remaining potatoes. Bake 5-10 minutes longer or until bubbly and potatoes are crisp. **Yield:** 4 servings.

Meatless

Picante Biscuit Bake, p. 81

Chapter 6

Southwestern Veggie Bake

(Pictured below)

Refrigerated corn bread twists create an appealing lattice top on this zippy main dish. The original recipe contained cooked chicken instead of kidney beans and celery, but my family prefers my meatless version, which is spicier, too.
—Julie Zeager, Kent, Ohio

    3 medium carrots, sliced
    2 celery ribs, chopped
    1 small onion, chopped
    2 to 3 teaspoons chili powder
    1 teaspoon ground cumin
  1/4 teaspoon cayenne pepper
    2 tablespoons butter
    3 tablespoons all-purpose flour
  1/2 cup milk
    1 can (16 ounces) kidney beans, rinsed
      and drained
    1 can (15 ounces) black beans, rinsed and
      drained
    1 can (15-1/4 ounces) whole kernel corn,
      drained
    1 can (14-1/2 ounces) diced tomatoes,
      undrained
    1 can (4 ounces) chopped green chilies
    1 tube (11-1/2 ounces) refrigerated corn
      bread twists

In a large skillet, saute the carrots, celery, onion and seasonings in butter until vegetables are crisp-tender. Stir in flour until blended. Gradually add the milk. Bring to a boil; cook and stir for 2 minutes or until thickened and bubbly. Remove from the heat; add beans, corn, tomatoes and chilies. Spoon into an ungreased 13-in. x 9-in. x 2-in. baking dish. Separate corn bread twists; weave a lattice crust over filling. Bake, uncovered, at 350° for 20-25 minutes or until corn bread is done. **Yield:** 8 servings.

Swiss Macaroni

I bring smiles to the faces of friends with my comforting combination of macaroni, onion and Swiss cheese. I enjoy sharing this casserole.
—Carolyn Steele, Marathon Shores, Florida

    1 package (7 ounces) elbow macaroni
    1 jar (2 ounces) diced pimientos, drained
    2 eggs, lightly beaten
    1 cup half-and-half cream
    1 small onion, chopped
    2 tablespoons minced fresh parsley
  1-1/2 teaspoons salt
  1/8 teaspoon pepper
    1 cup soft bread crumbs
    1 cup (4 ounces) shredded Swiss cheese
  1/4 cup butter, melted

Cook macaroni according to package directions; drain and place in a greased 11-in. x 7-in. x 2-in. baking dish. Stir in the pimientos. In a bowl, combine the eggs, cream, onion, parsley, salt and pepper. Pour over macaroni mixture. Sprinkle with bread crumbs and cheese; drizzle with butter. Bake, uncovered, at 350° for 30 minutes or until golden brown. **Yield:** 6-8 servings.

Chili Casserole

I threw together this main dish when my husband unexpectedly invited his hunting buddies for dinner. It was on the table by the time they'd unpacked their gear and washed up.
—Karen Bruggman, Edmonds, Washington

    1 can (40 ounces) chili with beans
    1 can (4 ounces) chopped green chilies
    1 can (2-1/4 ounces) sliced ripe olives,
      drained
    2 cups (8 ounces) shredded cheddar
      cheese
    2 cups ranch-flavored tortilla chips,
      crushed

In a bowl, combine all ingredients. Transfer to a greased 2-1/2-qt. baking dish. Bake, uncovered, at 350° for 30-35 minutes or until bubbly. **Yield:** 6 servings.

Black Bean Nacho Bake

Pasta, black beans and nacho cheese soup combine in this speedy six-ingredient supper.
—Melodie Gay, Salt Lake City, Utah

- 1 package (7 ounces) shell *or* elbow macaroni, cooked and drained
- 1 can (15 ounces) black beans, rinsed and drained
- 1 can (11 ounces) nacho cheese soup
- 1/3 cup milk
- 1/2 cup crushed tortilla chips
- 1/2 cup shredded cheddar cheese

In a bowl, combine macaroni and beans. Combine soup and milk; stir into macaroni mixture. Transfer to a greased 8-in. square baking dish. Cover and bake at 350° for 25 minutes. Uncover; sprinkle with tortilla chips and cheese. Bake 5-10 minutes longer or until cheese is melted. **Yield:** 4 servings.

Artichoke Spinach Shells

If you're looking for a vegetarian meal, this is wonderful as the main course. We like to serve it with hot dinner rolls and a salad. —*Rachel Balsamo Lewiston, Maine*

- 4 cups uncooked medium pasta shells
- 10 ounces fresh spinach, chopped
- 3 cups (12 ounces) shredded cheddar cheese
- 1 can (14-1/2 ounces) Italian stewed tomatoes
- 1 can (14 ounces) water-packed artichoke hearts, drained and quartered
- 1 cup (8 ounces) sour cream
- 1/2 teaspoon garlic salt

In a Dutch oven, cook pasta in boiling water for 5 minutes. Add spinach; cook, uncovered, for 6-8 minutes or until pasta is tender. Drain. In a large bowl, combine the remaining ingredients. Stir in pasta mixture until blended. Transfer to a 3-qt. baking dish. Bake, uncovered, at 350° for 30-35 minutes or until heated through. **Yield:** 6-8 servings.

Three-Cheese Spaghetti Bake

(Pictured above right)

I created this mild casserole that is such a hit there are never any leftovers. I serve it with a green salad and garlic bread. —*Laura Linder, Kenedy, Texas*

- 1 package (16 ounces) spaghetti
- 2 cups (8 ounces) shredded mozzarella cheese, *divided*
- 3/4 cup grated Parmesan cheese
- 1/2 cup grated Romano cheese
- 3 eggs, beaten
- 1 tablespoon olive oil
- 2 teaspoons garlic powder
- Salt and pepper to taste
- 1 jar (28 ounces) spaghetti sauce

Cook spaghetti according to package directions; drain. Add 1 cup mozzarella cheese, Parmesan, Romano, eggs, oil, garlic powder, salt and pepper. Press into a greased 13-in. x 9-in. x 2-in. baking dish. Top with spaghetti sauce. Cover and bake at 350° for 20 minutes.

Uncover; sprinkle with the remaining mozzarella. Bake 10 minutes longer or until heated through and cheese is melted. **Yield:** 6-8 servings.

Choosing Bakeware

For even cooking, try to bake the casserole in the dish size called for in the recipe. Round and oval baking dishes are identified by quart capacity. Square and oblong dishes are measured in inches across the top, from inside edge to inside edge.

crumbs. Cover with half of the zucchini, ricotta mixture and mozzarella. Repeat layers of sauce, zucchini, ricotta mixture and mozzarella. Cover with remaining sauce. Combine remaining crumbs and Parmesan; sprinkle over top.

Cover and bake at 350° for 45 minutes. Uncover; bake 15 minutes longer. Let stand 15 minutes before cutting. **Yield:** 12 servings.

Nutritional Analysis: One serving equals 201 calories, 237 mg sodium, 21 mg cholesterol, 18 g carbohydrate, 12 g protein, 9 g fat, 3 g fiber. **Diabetic Exchanges:** 1 starch, 1 meat, 1 fat, 1/2 vegetable.

Zucchini Ricotta Bake

(Pictured above)

I've made this lasagna-like zucchini casserole frequently over the years and shared the recipe with many. —*Eleanor Hauserman*
Huntsville, Alabama

✓ Uses less fat, sugar or salt. Includes Nutritional Analysis and Diabetic Exchanges.

  2 pounds zucchini
  1 carton (15 ounces) light ricotta cheese
Egg substitute equivalent to 2 eggs
  1/2 cup dry bread crumbs, *divided*
    5 tablespoons grated Parmesan cheese, *divided*
    1 tablespoon minced parsley
    1/4 teaspoon dried oregano
    1/4 teaspoon dried basil
    1/8 teaspoon pepper
    1 jar (26 ounces) reduced-sodium spaghetti sauce
1-1/2 cups (6 ounces) shredded part-skim reduced-fat mozzarella cheese

Cut zucchini lengthwise into 1/4-in. slices. Place in a basket over 1 in. of boiling water. Cover and steam 5-6 minutes or until just tender. Drain; pat dry.

In a bowl, combine ricotta, egg substitute, 3 tablespoons bread crumbs, 3 tablespoons Parmesan, parsley, oregano, basil and pepper; set aside. Spread a third of the spaghetti sauce in a 13-in. x 9-in. x 2-in. baking dish coated with nonstick cooking spray. Sprinkle with 2 tablespoons bread

Rice 'n' Black Bean Bake

When I come home from work, I start cooking the rice for this meatless casserole right away. The rest is a breeze, because it's just opening cans and mixing. —*Kathy Prado, Fort Worth, Texas*

  1 can (15 ounces) black beans, rinsed and drained
  1 can (10 ounces) diced tomatoes and green chilies, undrained
  1 can (8 ounces) tomato sauce
  1 jar (8 ounces) picante sauce
  2 cups cooked rice
  1 cup (8 ounces) sour cream
  2 cups (8 ounces) shredded cheddar cheese, *divided*
Corn *or* **tortilla chips**

In a bowl, combine the first four ingredients. Stir in the rice, sour cream and 1 cup of cheese. Transfer to a greased 13-in. x 9-in. x 2-in. baking dish. Sprinkle with the remaining cheese.

Bake, uncovered, at 350° for 20 minutes or until the cheese is melted. Serve with corn or tortilla chips. **Yield:** 6 servings.

Brown Rice Casserole

This hearty dish passes the test with my teenage boys, who can be finicky eaters. —*Glenda Schwarz*
Morden, Manitoba

  2 quarts water
1-1/2 cups uncooked brown rice
  1 cup dry split peas
  1 cup chopped fresh mushrooms
  2 celery ribs, chopped
  2 medium carrots, grated
  1 medium onion, chopped
  2 garlic cloves, minced

1 tablespoon vegetable oil
1 can (14-1/2 ounces) diced tomatoes,
    undrained
1/2 to 1 teaspoon salt
1/2 to 1 teaspoon dried thyme
1/2 to 1 teaspoon dried oregano
1/2 to 1 teaspoon pepper
1 cup (4 ounces) shredded cheddar
    cheese

In a large saucepan, bring water, rice and peas to a boil. Reduce heat; cover and simmer for 20-25 minutes or until tender. Drain and set aside.

In a skillet, saute the mushrooms, celery, carrots, onion and garlic in oil until vegetables are tender. Combine the vegetables, rice mixture, tomatoes and seasonings.

Transfer to a greased 2-1/2-qt. baking dish. Cover and bake at 350° for 30 minutes. Uncover; sprinkle with cheese. Bake 5-10 minutes longer or until the cheese is melted. **Yield:** 9 servings.

Picante Biscuit Bake

(Pictured on page 76)

To make this bake heartier, you can add a pound of cooked ground beef. Or try a pizza variation using pizza sauce, pepperoni and mozzarella cheese.
—Lanita Anderson, Jacksonville, North Carolina

2 tubes (12 ounces *each*) refrigerated
    buttermilk biscuits
1 jar (16 ounces) picante sauce *or* salsa
1 medium green pepper, chopped
1 medium onion, chopped
1 can (2-1/4 ounces) sliced ripe olives,
    drained
2 cups (8 ounces) shredded Monterey
    Jack cheese

Quarter the biscuits; place in a greased 13-in. x 9-in. x 2-in. baking dish. Top with picante sauce, green pepper, onion and olives. Bake, uncovered, at 350° for 20 minutes. Sprinkle with cheese. Bake 10 minutes longer or until the cheese is melted. **Yield:** 6 servings.

Tortellini Broccoli Bake

(Pictured at right)

This is a great main dish. Everyone, even my young granddaughters, enjoys the combination of broccoli, cheese and tortellini. —*Esther McCoy*
Dillonvale, Ohio

1 package (19 ounces) frozen cheese
    tortellini, cooked and drained
1 package (16 ounces) frozen chopped
    broccoli, thawed
1 jar (2 ounces) diced pimientos, drained
2 tablespoons chopped onion
CHEESE SAUCE:
1 garlic clove, minced
2 tablespoons butter
2 tablespoons all-purpose flour
1/4 teaspoon salt
1/8 teaspoon pepper
1/8 teaspoon ground nutmeg
1 cup milk
1/3 cup plus 1/4 cup grated Parmesan
    cheese, *divided*

In a large bowl, combine the tortellini, broccoli, pimientos and onion; set aside. In a saucepan, saute garlic in butter for 1 minute. Stir in the flour, salt, pepper and nutmeg. Gradually stir in milk until blended. Bring to a boil; cook and stir for 2 minutes or until thickened. Remove from the heat; stir in 1/3 cup Parmesan cheese until melted. Fold into broccoli mixture.

Transfer to a greased 2-qt. baking dish. Cover and bake at 350° for 40-45 minutes or until hot and bubbly, stirring twice. Top with remaining Parmesan. Cover and let stand for 5 minutes or until cheese is melted. **Yield:** 4-6 servings.

Ravioli Casserole

(Pictured below)

The whole family will love the fun, cheesy flavor of this main dish that tastes like lasagna without all the fuss. Time-saving ingredients, including prepared spaghetti sauce and frozen ravioli, hurry the preparation along.
—Mary Ann Rothert
Austin, Texas

> 1 jar (28 ounces) spaghetti sauce
> 1 package (25 ounces) frozen cheese ravioli, cooked and drained
> 2 cups (16 ounces) small-curd cottage cheese
> 4 cups (16 ounces) shredded mozzarella cheese
> 1/4 cup grated Parmesan cheese

Spread 1/2 cup of spaghetti sauce in an ungreased 13-in. x 9-in. x 2-in. baking dish. Layer with half of the ravioli, 1-1/4 cups of sauce, 1 cup of cottage cheese and 2 cups of mozzarella cheese. Repeat layers. Sprinkle with the Parmesan cheese.

Bake, uncovered, at 350° for 30-40 minutes or until bubbly. Let stand 5-10 minutes before serving. **Yield:** 6-8 servings.

Editor's Note: 4-5 cups of any style cooked ravioli may be substituted for the frozen cheese ravioli.

Carrot Lentil Casserole

My husband loves this hearty meatless casserole, especially on a chilly winter evening. It's wonderful served with crusty bread and a green salad.
—Stacey Krawczyk, Champaign, Illinois

 Uses less fat, sugar or salt. Includes Nutritional Analysis and Diabetic Exchanges.

> 1 large onion, chopped
> 1 cup finely chopped carrots
> 3/4 cup lentils, rinsed
> 3/4 cup uncooked brown rice
> 3/4 cup shredded reduced-fat cheddar cheese
> 1/2 cup chopped green pepper
> 1/2 teaspoon *each* dried thyme, basil and oregano
> 1/4 teaspoon salt
> 1/4 teaspoon rubbed sage
> 1/4 teaspoon garlic powder
> 1 can (14-1/2 ounces) chicken *or* vegetable broth
> 1 can (14-1/2 ounces) diced tomatoes, undrained

In a 1-1/2-qt. baking dish coated with nonstick cooking spray, combine the onion, carrots, lentils, rice, cheese, green pepper and seasonings. Stir in broth and tomatoes. Cover and bake at 350° for 1 to 1-1/2 hours or until the liquid is absorbed and lentils and rice are tender. **Yield:** 6 servings.

Nutritional Analysis: One serving (1 cup) equals 239 calories, 4 g fat (2 g saturated fat), 8 mg cholesterol, 557 mg sodium, 41 g carbohydrate, 8 g fiber, 14 g protein. **Diabetic Exchanges:** 2 starch, 1 lean meat, 1 vegetable.

Six-Veggie Bake

I altered the original recipe for this strata-like dish and replaced the sausage with fresh vegetables.
—Kate Hilts, Fairbanks, Alaska

 Uses less fat, sugar or salt. Includes Nutritional Analysis and Diabetic Exchanges.

> 1 loaf (1 pound) Italian bread, cut into 1/2-inch cubes
> 1 can (14-1/2 ounces) diced tomatoes, undrained
> 1 package (10 ounces) frozen chopped spinach, thawed and well drained
> 1 cup chopped fresh mushrooms
> 1 cup (4 ounces) shredded part-skim mozzarella cheese
> 1/2 cup chopped green pepper
> 1/2 cup chopped zucchini
> 2 green onions, chopped

1 teaspoon dried basil
1/2 teaspoon dried oregano
1 cup fat-free milk
Egg substitute equivalent to 4 eggs
1 teaspoon salt-free seasoning blend
1/4 teaspoon pepper

In a large bowl, combine the first 10 ingredients; mix well. Place in a 13-in. x 9-in. x 2-in. baking dish coated with nonstick cooking spray. In a small bowl, combine milk, egg substitute, seasoning blend and pepper; pour over the vegetable mixture. Cover and refrigerate for 2 hours or overnight.

Remove from the refrigerator 30 minutes before baking. Cover and bake at 425° for 15 minutes. Uncover; bake 15 minutes longer or until a knife inserted near the center comes out clean. **Yield:** 16 servings.

Nutritional Analysis: One serving equals 128 calories, 292 mg sodium, 5 mg cholesterol, 18 g carbohydrate, 8 g protein, 3 g fat, 2 g fiber. **Diabetic Exchanges:** 1 starch, 1 vegetable, 1/2 meat.

Oregano Potato Casserole

Seasonings, cottage cheese, sour cream and eggs dress up ordinary mashed potatoes in this casserole. —*Barbara Stewart, Portland, Connecticut*

2-1/2 cups mashed potatoes (prepared with
    milk)
  1 cup (8 ounces) small-curd cottage
    cheese
1/2 cup sour cream
  3 eggs, *separated*
  2 tablespoons minced fresh oregano *or* 2
    teaspoons dried oregano
  2 tablespoons minced fresh parsley *or* 2
    teaspoons dried parsley flakes
1/2 teaspoon seasoned salt
  2 tablespoons butter

In a large bowl, combine the potatoes, cottage cheese, sour cream, egg yolks, oregano, parsley and seasoned salt. In a mixing bowl, beat egg whites until stiff peaks form; fold into potato mixture.

Transfer to a lightly greased 2-1/2-qt. baking dish. Dot with butter. Bake, uncovered, at 350° for 1 hour or until lightly browned. **Yield:** 6-8 servings.

Italian Bow Tie Bake

(Pictured above right)

Served with a green salad and garlic bread, this is the easiest dinner I prepare for my family. They love

the four-ingredient main dish and think I worked on it for hours. They don't even miss the meat!
    —*Lisa Blackwell, Henderson, North Carolina*

8 ounces uncooked bow tie pasta
1 jar (16 ounces) garlic and onion
    spaghetti sauce
1 envelope Italian salad dressing mix
2 cups (8 ounces) shredded mozzarella
    cheese

Cook pasta according to package directions; drain. In a bowl, combine the spaghetti sauce and salad dressing mix; add pasta and toss to coat. Transfer to a greased shallow 2-qt. baking dish. Sprinkle with cheese. Bake, uncovered, at 400° for 15-20 minutes or until heated through. **Yield:** 4 servings.

Fresh Herb Facts

Kitchen shears are great for snipping fresh herbs into small pieces. It's always best to use restraint when adding any herb to a dish. The flavor of an herb—oregano, for example—can vary widely depending on the variety and season. You can always add more, but it is hard to salvage an over-seasoned dish.

1 package (16 ounces) rigatoni *or* large
  tube pasta
2 tablespoons butter
1/4 cup all-purpose flour
1/2 teaspoon salt
2 cups milk
1/4 cup water
4 eggs, beaten
2 cans (8 ounces *each*) tomato sauce
2 cups (8 ounces) shredded mozzarella
  cheese
1/4 cup grated Parmesan cheese

Cook pasta according to package directions. Meanwhile, in a saucepan, melt butter. Stir in flour and salt until smooth; gradually add milk and water. Bring to a boil; cook and stir for 2 minutes or until thickened.

Drain pasta; place in a large bowl. Add eggs. Spoon into two greased 8-in. square baking dishes. Top each with one can of tomato sauce and 1 cup mozzarella cheese. Spoon white sauce over top; sprinkle with Parmesan cheese.

Cover and freeze one casserole for up to 3 months. Bake second casserole, uncovered, at 375° for 30-35 minutes or until a meat thermometer reads 160°.

To use frozen casserole: Thaw in the refrigerator overnight. Remove from refrigerator 30 minutes before baking. Cover and bake at 375° for 40 minutes. Uncover; bake 7-10 minutes longer or until a meat thermometer reads 160°. **Yield:** 2 casseroles (6-8 servings each).

Pinto Beans and Rice

(Pictured above)

I serve this at many potlucks and am asked for the recipe every time! —Linda Romano
Mt. Airy, North Carolina

1 large onion, chopped
2 tablespoons vegetable oil
3/4 cup ketchup
2 to 4 tablespoons brown sugar
1 teaspoon prepared mustard
1 teaspoon Liquid Smoke, optional
1 teaspoon salt
1/4 teaspoon pepper
3 cups cooked long grain rice
2 cans (15 ounces *each*) pinto beans,
  rinsed and drained

In a large skillet, saute onion in oil until tender. Remove from the heat; stir in ketchup, brown sugar, mustard, Liquid Smoke if desired, salt and pepper. Stir in rice and beans. Transfer to a greased 1-1/2-qt. baking dish. Bake, uncovered, at 350° for 30-35 minutes or until heated through. **Yield:** 6 servings.

Cheesy Rigatoni Bake

This is a family favorite. One of our four children always asks for it as a birthday dinner.
—Nancy Urbine, Lancaster, Ohio

Baked Ziti

Many of my casserole recipes have been frowned upon by my children, but they give a cheer when they hear we're having Baked Ziti for supper.
—Charity Burkholder, Pittsboro, Indiana

3 cups uncooked ziti *or* small tube pasta
1-3/4 cups meatless spaghetti sauce, *divided*
1 cup (8 ounces) small-curd cottage
  cheese
1-1/2 cups (6 ounces) shredded mozzarella
  cheese, *divided*
1 egg, lightly beaten
2 teaspoons dried parsley flakes
1/2 teaspoon dried oregano
1/4 teaspoon garlic powder
1/8 teaspoon pepper

Cook pasta according to package directions. Meanwhile, in a large bowl, combine 3/4 cup spaghetti sauce, cottage cheese, 1 cup mozzarella cheese, egg, parsley, oregano, garlic powder and pepper. Drain pasta; stir into cheese mixture.

In a greased 8-in. square baking dish, spread 1/4

cup of spaghetti sauce. Top with pasta mixture, and remaining sauce and mozzarella. Cover and bake at 375° for 45 minutes. Uncover; bake 5-10 minutes longer or until bubbly. **Yield:** 6 servings.

Grilled Cheese in a Pan

My cousin served this dish at a shower years ago, and my daughter and I immediately asked for the recipe. If you don't have the exact cheeses it calls for, you can switch a couple and it still tastes absolutely delicious.
— *Mary Ann Wendt*
Ada, Michigan

1 tube (8 ounces) refrigerated crescent rolls
4 cups (1 cup *each*) shredded Muenster, Monterey Jack, Swiss and cheddar cheese
1 package (8 ounces) cream cheese, sliced
1 egg, lightly beaten
1 tablespoon butter, melted
1 tablespoon sesame seeds

Unroll crescent roll dough; divide in half. Seal perforations. Line an ungreased 8-in. square baking pan with half of the dough. Layer with the Muenster, Monterey Jack, Swiss, cheddar and cream cheese. Pour egg over all.

Top with remaining dough. Brush with butter; sprinkle with sesame seeds. Bake, uncovered, at 350° for 30-35 minutes or until golden brown. **Yield:** 9 servings.

Pierogi Casserole

My husband never tires of this hearty casserole, no matter how many times I serve it. It's great for potlucks, too.
— *Margaret Popou*
Kaslo, British Columbia

1 cup finely chopped onion
1/4 cup butter
2 cups small-curd cottage cheese, drained
1 egg
1/4 teaspoon onion salt
2 cups mashed potatoes (prepared with milk and butter)
1 cup (4 ounces) shredded cheddar cheese
1/4 teaspoon salt
1/8 teaspoon pepper
9 lasagna noodles, cooked and drained

In a skillet, saute onion in butter until tender; set aside. In a bowl, combine cottage cheese, egg and

onion salt. In another bowl, combine potatoes, cheddar cheese, salt and pepper.

Place three noodles in a greased 13-in. x 9-in. x 2-in. baking dish. Top with cottage cheese mixture and three more noodles. Top with potato mixture, remaining noodles and sauteed onion. Cover and bake at 350° for 25-30 minutes or until heated through. Let stand 10 minutes before serving. **Yield:** 12 servings.

Meatless Chili Bake

(Pictured below)

My husband is a farmer, and this delicious dish is easy and quick to fix whenever he decides to come in and eat. Our children all like it, too.
— *Lisa Flamme, Gladbrook, Iowa*

2-1/2 cups uncooked spiral pasta
1 can (15 ounces) vegetarian chili with beans
1 jar (12 ounces) chunky salsa
1 can (11 ounces) whole kernel corn, drained
1/2 cup shredded cheddar cheese

Cook pasta according to package directions; drain. In a large bowl, combine the chili, salsa and corn. Add pasta; toss to coat. Transfer to a greased shallow 2-qt. baking dish; sprinkle with cheese. Bake, uncovered, at 400° for 25-30 minutes or until bubbly. **Yield:** 4-6 servings.

cup cheddar cheese and Parmesan cheese. Transfer to a greased 9-in. springform pan. Place pan on a baking sheet.

Bake, uncovered, at 350° for 25 minutes. Sprinkle with remaining cheddar cheese. Bake 5-10 minutes longer or until a knife inserted near the center comes out clean. Let stand for 10 minutes. Run a knife around edge of pan to loosen; remove sides. Cut into wedges. **Yield:** 6-8 servings.

Vegetable Noodle Bake

(Pictured below)

Traditional lasagna fixings make up this casserole. Egg noodles are a great substitute for the usual lasagna noodles. —*Dixie Terry, Goreville, Illinois*

> 1 can (14-1/2 ounces) whole tomatoes, drained and cut up
> 3/4 cup canned tomato puree
> 1/3 cup chopped onion
> 1-1/4 teaspoons dried oregano
> 1/4 teaspoon garlic powder
> 1/4 teaspoon salt
> 1/8 teaspoon pepper
> 2-1/2 cups uncooked medium egg noodles
> 1/2 cup small-curd cottage cheese
> 1 package (10 ounces) frozen chopped spinach, thawed and squeezed dry
> 1/3 cup shredded American cheese

In a large saucepan, combine the tomatoes, tomato puree, onion, oregano, garlic powder, salt and pepper. Bring to a boil. Reduce heat; simmer, un-

Confetti Spaghetti Pie

(Pictured above)

Getting everyone to the dinner table is never a problem when I bake up this great pie. It's filling, plus it's packed with veggies. —*Ruth Lee, Troy, Ontario*

> 1 package (7 ounces) spaghetti
> 1 medium onion, chopped
> 2 garlic cloves, minced
> 2 tablespoons vegetable oil
> 2 medium tomatoes, chopped
> 3 tablespoons tomato paste
> 1/4 cup minced fresh parsley
> 1/2 teaspoon dried oregano
> 1/2 to 1 teaspoon salt
> 1/4 teaspoon pepper
> 4 eggs, lightly beaten
> 1/2 cup frozen peas, thawed
> 1/2 cup frozen cut green beans, thawed
> 1/2 cup chopped fresh broccoli
> 1 cup (4 ounces) shredded cheddar cheese, *divided*
> 1/4 cup grated Parmesan cheese

Break spaghetti in half; cook according to package directions. Drain and rinse in cold water; set aside. In a skillet, saute onion and garlic in oil until tender. Stir in the tomatoes, tomato paste, parsley, oregano, salt and pepper. Cook until heated through, about 5 minutes.

In a large bowl, toss the spaghetti and eggs. Stir in peas, beans, broccoli, tomato mixture, 1/4

covered, for 15 minutes. Meanwhile, cook noodles according to package directions; drain.

Spread 1/3 cup tomato mixture in a greased shallow 2-qt. baking dish. Top with half of the noodles. Spread with cottage cheese; top with spinach. Drizzle with 1/2 cup tomato mixture; top with remaining noodles and tomato mixture. Sprinkle with American cheese. Cover and bake at 350° for 20-25 minutes or until cheese is melted. **Yield:** 4 servings.

Four-Veggie Casserole

Several members of my family enjoy meatless dishes, and I'm partial to casseroles, so this tasty dish pleases everyone. —Ruby Williams
Bogalusa, Louisiana

  3 medium zucchini, cut into 1/4-inch slices
  1 pound fresh mushrooms, sliced
  1 medium onion, chopped
1/2 cup chopped green onions
  8 tablespoons butter, *divided*
1/4 cup all-purpose flour
  1 cup milk
  1 can (14 ounces) water-packed
    artichokes, drained and quartered
3/4 cup shredded Swiss cheese
1/2 teaspoon salt
1/4 teaspoon pepper
3/4 cup seasoned bread crumbs

In a large skillet, saute the zucchini, mushrooms and onions in 3 tablespoons butter until zucchini is crisp-tender; remove and set aside. In the same skillet, melt 3 tablespoons butter. Stir in flour until smooth. Gradually stir in milk until blended. Bring to a boil; cook and stir for 2 minutes or until thickened. Stir in the zucchini mixture, artichokes, cheese, salt and pepper; mix well.

Transfer to a greased 11-in. x 7-in. x 2-in. baking dish. Melt remaining butter; toss with bread crumbs. Sprinkle over the top. Bake, uncovered, at 350° for 20-25 minutes or until bubbly and topping is lightly browned. **Yield:** 8 servings.

Pizza Pasta Pie

(Pictured above right)

I received this recipe years ago. When I try a new recipe and like it, I write the date, who was at the meal and any comments about the dish right on the card. That makes it fun when I go back through my recipes later. —Harriet Stichter
Milford, Indiana

  2 eggs
1-1/2 cups cooked spaghetti
  4 tablespoons grated Parmesan cheese,
    divided
  1 tablespoon butter, melted
  1 package (10 ounces) frozen chopped
    spinach, thawed and squeezed dry
3/4 cup small-curd cottage cheese
  1 cup pizza sauce
1/2 cup finely shredded carrot
1/4 cup chopped fresh mushrooms
  1 teaspoon dried oregano
1/2 teaspoon dried basil
1/4 teaspoon garlic powder
1/2 cup shredded mozzarella cheese

In a bowl, beat one egg. Stir in the spaghetti, 2 tablespoons Parmesan cheese and butter; mix well. Spread onto the bottom and up the sides of a greased 9-in. pie plate. Spread spinach over top.

In a bowl, lightly beat the remaining egg. Stir in cottage cheese and remaining Parmesan. Spread over spinach. Combine pizza sauce, carrot, mushrooms, oregano, basil and garlic powder; pour over cottage cheese mixture.

Bake, uncovered, at 350° for 25-30 minutes. Sprinkle with mozzarella cheese; bake 5 minutes longer or until cheese is melted. Let stand for 5 minutes before cutting. **Yield:** 6 servings.

Side Dishes

Apple-a-Day Casserole, p. 98

Chapter 7

Swiss Potato Kugel

(Pictured below)

I've enjoyed cooking and baking ever since I was small. I thoroughly enjoy planning a sumptuous dinner for my family. We have a daughter who loves potatoes of any kind. I believe she could eat this dish and pass over all the other goodies on the table.
—Judy Wilson, Placentia, California

- 1 cup finely chopped onion
- 2 tablespoons butter
- 4 cups shredded *or* diced cooked peeled potatoes (about 4 medium)
- 2 cups (8 ounces) shredded Swiss cheese
- 1/4 cup all-purpose flour
- 1 teaspoon salt
- 1/4 teaspoon pepper
- 3 eggs
- 3/4 cup half-and-half cream
- Tomato slices and fresh thyme, optional

In a large skillet, saute onion in butter until tender. Remove from the heat; add potatoes. Toss cheese with flour, salt and pepper; add to skillet and blend well. In a small bowl, combine the eggs and cream. Stir into the potato mixture.

Spoon into a greased 9-in. square baking dish. Bake, uncovered, at 350° for 20-30 minutes or until golden brown. Cool for 5 minutes; cut into squares. Garnish with tomato and thyme if desired. **Yield:** 9 servings.

Editor's Note: This recipe can be prepared the day before, covered and refrigerated overnight. Remove from the refrigerator 30 minutes before baking. Bake for 30-40 minutes.

Autumn Squash Bake

The sweetness of pears and tangy flavor of cranberries really complement the squash. This dish has become a favorite at family holiday meals.
—Patty Baumann, Savannah, Missouri

 Uses less fat, sugar or salt. Includes Nutritional Analysis and Diabetic Exchanges.

- 9 cups diced peeled Hubbard squash
- 2 medium pears, cut into 1-inch pieces
- 1 cup fresh *or* frozen cranberries
- 1 tablespoon margarine
- 2 tablespoons water

Combine all ingredients in a 3-qt. baking dish coated with nonstick cooking spray. Cover and bake at 350° for 50-55 minutes or until squash is tender. **Yield:** 14 servings.

Nutritional Analysis: One serving (3/4 cup) equals 102 calories, 22 mg sodium, 0 cholesterol, 21 g carbohydrate, 4 g protein, 2 g fat, 5 g fiber. **Diabetic Exchanges:** 1 starch, 1/2 fruit.

Spinach Rice Bake

Lenexa became known as the spinach capital of the world back in the 1930s when Belgian farmers around here raised and sold tons of that leafy crop. Every September, the community celebrates this heritage. Since Kansas was once considered the "jumping off" point for the Oregon Trail and the Sante Fe Trail, we hold 1800s reenactments with food and craft booths and, of course, a spinach recipe contest. This recipe is a favorite.
—Kathy Kittell
Lenexa, Kansas

- 1 package (10 ounces) frozen chopped spinach
- 1 cup cooked long grain rice
- 1 cup (4 ounces) shredded cheddar cheese
- 2 eggs, lightly beaten
- 1/3 cup milk
- 3 tablespoons finely chopped onion
- 2 tablespoons minced fresh parsley
- 2 tablespoons butter, softened
- 1/2 teaspoon salt
- 1/2 teaspoon Worcestershire sauce
- 1/4 teaspoon dried thyme
- 1/8 to 1/4 teaspoon ground nutmeg

Cook spinach according to package directions; drain well. Add the remaining ingredients; mix well. Transfer to a greased 1-qt. baking dish. Cover and bake at 350° for 20 minutes. Uncover; bake 20-25 minutes longer or until a knife inserted near the center comes out clean. **Yield:** 4 servings.

Mozzarella Tomatoes

I received the recipe for this rich bread-and-tomato dish from a relative. We love it in fall when tomatoes from our garden are plentiful. It's a favorite at potlucks, too. —Gloria Bisek
Deerwood, Minnesota

- **4 medium tomatoes, sliced**
- **8 cups soft bread cubes**
- **3 cups (12 ounces) shredded mozzarella cheese, *divided***
- **4 bacon strips, cooked and crumbled**
- **1/2 cup butter, melted**
- **1/2 cup chopped celery**
- **1/2 cup chopped onion**
- **2 eggs, beaten**
- **1/2 teaspoon garlic salt**
- **1/2 teaspoon dried oregano**

Place a single layer of tomatoes in a greased 13-in. x 9-in. x 2-in. baking dish; set aside. In a large bowl, combine bread cubes, 2 cups of cheese, bacon, butter, celery, onion, eggs, garlic salt and oregano; mix well.

Spoon over the tomatoes. Top with remaining tomatoes; sprinkle with remaining cheese. Bake, uncovered, at 350° for 30 minutes or until heated through. **Yield:** 6-8 servings.

Broccoli Cauliflower Bake

(Pictured above right)

Guests always ask for the recipe whenever I serve these vegetables. And because this dish is so easy to prepare, I have plenty of time to finish up the rest of our dinner. —Erika Anderson
Wausau, Wisconsin

- **1 medium head cauliflower, broken into small florets**
- **1 pound fresh broccoli, broken into small florets**
- **1-1/2 cups shredded Monterey Jack cheese**
- **1 cup (8 ounces) sour cream**
- **1 can (4 ounces) chopped green chilies, drained**
- **4 tablespoons butter, melted, *divided***
- **1 teaspoon salt**
- **1/4 teaspoon pepper**
- **3/4 cup crushed seasoned stuffing**

Add 1 in. of water to a Dutch oven; add cauliflower and broccoli. Bring to a boil. Reduce heat; cover and cook for 7 minutes or until tender.

Meanwhile, in a bowl, combine the cheese, sour cream, chilies, 2 tablespoons butter, salt and pepper. Drain vegetables well; gently fold in cheese mixture.

Transfer to a greased 2-1/2-qt. baking dish. Toss stuffing and remaining butter; sprinkle over vegetables. Bake, uncovered, at 350° for 20-25 minutes or until heated through. **Yield:** 6-8 servings.

Cutting Time

To save prep time later, chop several onions and green peppers in advance. Store separately in resealable freezer bags. When you need chopped vegetables for a casserole, just measure the amount called for, reseal the bag and return it to the freezer. Commercially cut and frozen onions and green peppers are also available in the frozen food section of supermarkets.

pepper, cheese and bread crumbs. Melt remaining butter; pour over the top. Bake, uncovered, at 375° for 20 minutes or until heated through. **Yield:** 8 servings.

Colorful Veggie Bake

(Pictured below)

It's impossible to resist this cheesy casserole with a golden crumb topping sprinkled over colorful vegetables. —Lisa Radelet, Boulder, Colorado

> **2 packages (16 ounces *each*) frozen California-blend vegetables**
> **8 ounces process cheese (Velveeta), cubed**
> **6 tablespoons butter, *divided***
> **1/2 cup crushed butter-flavored crackers (about 13 crackers)**

Prepare vegetables according to package directions; drain. Place half in an ungreased 11-in. x 7-in. x 2-in. baking dish. In a small saucepan, combine cheese and 4 tablespoons butter; cook and stir over low heat until melted. Pour half over vegetables. Repeat layers.

Melt the remaining butter; toss with cracker

Broccoli Bean Bake

(Pictured above)

This may sound like an unusual combination, but it's a tasty way to get my husband and son to eat broccoli. —Valerie McInroy, Waterloo, Iowa

> **6 cups broccoli florets (about 1 large bunch)**
> **1 small onion, chopped**
> **2 garlic cloves, minced**
> **3 tablespoons butter, *divided***
> **1 can (15-1/2 ounces) great northern beans, rinsed and drained**
> **1 jar (4 ounces) diced pimientos, drained**
> **1 teaspoon dried oregano**
> **1/2 teaspoon salt**
> **1/8 teaspoon pepper**
> **2 cups (8 ounces) shredded cheddar cheese**
> **3 tablespoons dry bread crumbs**

Place broccoli in a saucepan; add 1 in. of water. Bring to a boil. Reduce heat; cover and simmer for 5-8 minutes or until crisp-tender. Meanwhile, in a skillet, saute onion and garlic in 1 tablespoon butter. Spread in a greased 11-in. x 7-in. x 2-in. baking dish.

Drain broccoli; place over onion mixture. Top with beans and pimientos. Sprinkle with oregano, salt,

crumbs. Sprinkle over the top. Bake, uncovered, at 325° for 20-25 minutes or until golden brown. **Yield:** 8-10 servings.

Creamy Asparagus Casserole

Unlike most kids, my son doesn't consider aspara-gus "yucky"—he loves it! Whenever I serve this dish, there's never any left. —Teresa Kachermeyer
Frederick, Maryland

  1 can (10-3/4 ounces) condensed creamy
    chicken mushroom soup, undiluted
1/2 cup milk
  1 package (10 ounces) frozen cut green
    beans, thawed
  1 package (8 ounces) frozen asparagus
    cuts and tips, thawed and drained
  1 can (4 ounces) mushroom stems and
    pieces, drained
  2 cups cubed day-old bread
  2 tablespoons sliced almonds
  2 tablespoons butter, melted

In a large bowl, combine soup and milk. Add beans, asparagus and mushrooms; mix well. Pour into a greased 8-in. square baking dish. Cover and bake at 350° for 20 minutes.

Toss the bread cubes, almonds and butter and sprinkle over the casserole. Bake, uncovered, 15-20 minutes longer or until bubbly. **Yield:** 6-8 servings.

Mushroom Corn Casserole

I decided to create a casserole that combined corn, mushrooms and a rich cheesy sauce. I succeeded with this recipe. It's an easy dish to make and a pop-ular part of any party buffet. —Mary Jones
Cumberland, Maine

1/3 cup chopped green pepper
1/3 cup finely chopped onion
  3 tablespoons butter, *divided*
1/4 cup all-purpose flour
  1 can (14-3/4 ounces) cream-style corn
1/2 teaspoon salt
1/8 teaspoon pepper
  1 package (3 ounces) cream cheese,
    cubed
  1 can (15-1/4 ounces) whole kernel corn,
    drained
  1 can (4 ounces) mushroom stems and
    pieces, drained

1/2 cup shredded Swiss cheese
1-1/2 cups soft bread crumbs

In a saucepan, saute green pepper and onion in 1 tablespoon butter until tender. Stir in flour, cream corn, salt and pepper until blended. Add cream cheese; stir until melted. Stir in the whole kernel corn, mushrooms and Swiss cheese. Transfer to a greased 1-1/2-qt. baking dish. Melt remaining but-ter; toss with bread crumbs. Sprinkle over the corn mixture. Bake, uncovered, at 400° for 20-25 min-utes or until heated through. **Yield:** 4-6 servings.

Almond Celery Bake

(Pictured above)

It took a creative cook like Mom to find a way to make celery star in a satisfying side dish.
—Judi Messina, Coeur d'Alene, Idaho

  1 bunch celery, sliced (about 6 cups)
3/4 cup shredded cheddar cheese
1/2 teaspoon paprika
1/8 teaspoon pepper
  1 can (10-3/4 ounces) condensed cream of
    celery soup, undiluted
  1 cup soft bread crumbs
1/2 cup slivered almonds

Place the celery in a greased 2-qt. baking dish. Sprinkle with cheese, paprika and pepper. Top with the soup. Sprinkle with bread crumbs. Cover and bake at 375° for 45 minutes. Uncover; sprinkle with the almonds. Bake 10-15 minutes longer or un-til golden brown. **Yield:** 10-12 servings.

South Coast Hominy

(Pictured below)

The first time I tasted this dish, I couldn't eat enough. It's something my stepmother has prepared for a long time. Whenever I fix it for my own family, there are never any leftovers. —Leslie Hampel Palmer, Texas

1/2 cup chopped onion
1/2 cup chopped green pepper
5 tablespoons butter, *divided*
3 tablespoons all-purpose flour
1 teaspoon salt
1/2 teaspoon ground mustard
Dash cayenne pepper
1-1/2 cups milk
1 cup (4 ounces) shredded cheddar cheese
1 can (15-1/2 ounces) white hominy, drained
1/2 cup sliced ripe olives, optional
1/2 cup dry bread crumbs

In a skillet, saute onion and green pepper in 3 tablespoons butter until tender. Add flour, salt, mustard and cayenne; cook and stir until smooth and bubbly, about 2 minutes. Gradually add milk; bring to a boil. Boil for 2 minutes, stirring constantly. Stir in cheese until melted. Remove from the heat; add hominy and olives if desired.

Pour into a greased 1-1/2-qt. baking dish. Melt remaining butter and toss with bread crumbs; sprinkle over hominy mixture. Bake, uncovered, at 375° for 30 minutes or until golden brown. **Yield:** 6-8 servings.

Deluxe Macaroni 'n' Cheese

We first tasted this dish while visiting my brother, Albert, in Huntsville, Alabama several years ago. Our grandchildren think any meal is incomplete without macaroni and cheese. My creamy "deluxe" version meets the approval of everyone at the table. —Bertha Johnson, Indianapolis, Indiana

2 cups small-curd cottage cheese
1 cup (8 ounces) sour cream
1 egg, lightly beaten
3/4 teaspoon salt
Garlic salt and pepper to taste
2 cups (8 ounces) shredded sharp cheddar cheese
1 package (7 ounces) elbow macaroni, cooked and drained
Paprika, optional

In a large bowl, combine the cottage cheese, sour cream, egg, salt, garlic salt and pepper. Add cheddar cheese; mix well. Add macaroni and stir until coated.

Transfer to a greased 2-1/2-qt. baking dish. Bake, uncovered, at 350° for 25-30 minutes or until heated through. Sprinkle with paprika if desired. **Yield:** 8-10 servings.

Apricot Barley Casserole

It doesn't take long to put together this pretty side dish dotted with dried apricots and golden raisins. Then just pop it into the oven and enjoy the aroma! —Diane Swink, Signal Mountain, Tennessee

2/3 cup pine nuts *or* slivered almonds
1/4 cup butter, *divided*
2 cups medium pearl barley
1 cup sliced green onions
7 cups chicken broth
2/3 cup diced dried apricots
1/2 cup golden raisins

In a skillet, saute nuts in 2 tablespoons butter until lightly browned; remove and set aside. In the same skillet, saute the barley and onions in remaining butter until onions are tender. Add broth; bring to a boil. Stir in the apricots, raisins and nuts. Pour into a greased 13-in. x 9-in. x 2-in. baking dish. Bake, uncovered, at 325° for 1-1/4 hours or until barley is tender. **Yield:** 8-10 servings.

Broccoli Casserole

Special enough for company, this colorful side dish is one my mom fixes often for Christmas dinner. The broccoli is baked with a rich creamy sauce, and cheese-flavored cracker crumbs are sprinkled over the top.
—Cindy Kufeldt
Orlando, Florida

   2 pounds fresh broccoli, cut into florets
   1 can (10-3/4 ounces) condensed cream of
      mushroom soup, undiluted
   1/2 cup mayonnaise
   1/2 cup shredded cheddar cheese
   1 tablespoon lemon juice
   1 cup crushed cheese-flavored snack
      crackers

Place 1 in. of water and broccoli in a saucepan; bring to a boil. Reduce heat; cover and simmer for 5-8 minutes or just until the broccoli is crisp-tender. Drain and place broccoli in a greased 2-qt. baking dish.

In a bowl, combine the soup, mayonnaise, cheese and lemon juice. Pour over broccoli. Sprinkle with crushed crackers. Bake, uncovered, at 350° for 25-30 minutes or until heated through. **Yield:** 6-8 servings.

   Editor's Note: Reduced-fat or fat-free mayonnaise is not recommended for this recipe.

Cheddar Cabbage Casserole

(Pictured above right)

Even those who generally don't care for cooked cabbage seem to like it this way—in a creamy sauce, topped with cheese and bread crumbs. The recipe was given to me by a friend, and everyone always wants seconds. It's cabbage at its best!
—Mildred Fowler, Thomaston, Georgia

   1 large head cabbage, shredded
   10 tablespoons butter, softened, *divided*
   1/4 cup all-purpose flour
   1/2 teaspoon salt
   1/8 teaspoon pepper
   4 cups milk

   2 cups (8 ounces) shredded cheddar
      cheese
   1 cup soft bread crumbs

In a large kettle, cook cabbage in boiling salted water for 2-3 minutes or until crisp-tender; drain well. Add 2 tablespoons butter; set aside.

In a small saucepan, melt 6 tablespoons butter; stir in flour, salt and pepper until smooth. Gradually add milk. Bring to a boil; cook and stir for 2 minutes or until thickened.

In a greased 3-qt. or 13-in. x 9-in. x 2-in. baking dish, place half of the cabbage. Pour half of the sauce over cabbage. Repeat layers. Sprinkle with cheese. Melt remaining butter; toss with bread crumbs. Sprinkle over cheese. Bake, uncovered, at 350° for 18-22 minutes or until cheese is melted. **Yield:** 12 servings.

About Broccoli

Buy broccoli with a deep, strong color— green or green tinged with purple. The quicker you cook broccoli, the greener it will remain. When using broccoli in stir-fries, casseroles or other dishes with mixed foods, boil it for a few minutes, cooling immediately in ice water to stop the cooking.

Italian Zucchini Casserole

(Pictured above)

Compliments crop up as fast as zucchini vines when folks sample this casserole.—Kimberly Speta
Kennedy, New York

     3 medium zucchini, sliced (about 6-1/2 cups)
     3 tablespoons olive oil, *divided*
     1 medium onion, sliced
     1 garlic clove, minced
     1 can (28 ounces) diced tomatoes, undrained
     1 tablespoon minced fresh basil *or* 1 teaspoon dried basil
 1-1/2 teaspoons minced fresh oregano *or* 1/2 teaspoon dried oregano
     1/2 teaspoon garlic salt
     1/4 teaspoon pepper
 1-1/2 cups dry instant stuffing mix
     1/2 cup grated Parmesan cheese
     3/4 cup shredded mozzarella cheese

In a large skillet, cook zucchini in 1 tablespoon oil until tender, about 5-6 minutes; drain and set aside. In the same skillet, saute the onion and garlic in remaining oil for 1 minute. Add tomatoes, basil, oregano, garlic salt and pepper; simmer, uncovered, for 10 minutes. Remove from the heat; gently stir in zucchini.

Place in an ungreased 13-in. x 9-in. x 2-in. baking dish. Top with stuffing mix; sprinkle with Parmesan cheese. Cover and bake at 350° for 20 minutes.

Uncover and sprinkle with mozzarella cheese. Return to the oven for 10 minutes or until golden. **Yield:** 6-8 servings.

Scalloped Turnips

(Pictured below)

My husband and I have five grown children and 13 grandchildren. This is the only kind of cooked turnips our kids will eat.   —Mrs. Eldon Larabee
Clearmont, Missouri

☑ Uses less fat, sugar or salt. Includes Nutritional Analysis and Diabetic Exchanges.

     3 cups diced peeled turnips
     2 cups water
     1 teaspoon sugar
     2 tablespoons butter
     3 tablespoons all-purpose flour
     3/4 teaspoon salt, optional
 1-1/2 cups milk
     1/4 cup crushed cornflakes
     2 tablespoons grated cheddar *or* Parmesan cheese, optional
Chopped fresh parsley, optional

Place the turnips, water and sugar in a saucepan; simmer for 5-8 minutes or until tender. Drain and set aside. In another saucepan, melt butter; stir in flour and salt if desired. Gradually add milk; bring to a boil. Cook and stir for 1-2 minutes. Stir in turnips. Pour into a greased 1-qt. baking dish; sprinkle

with cornflakes and cheese. Bake, uncovered, at 350° for 20 minutes or until bubbly. Garnish with parsley if desired. **Yield:** 5 servings.

Nutritional Analysis: One serving (prepared with margarine and fat-free milk and without salt) equals 128 calories, 187 mg sodium, 1 mg cholesterol, 18 g carbohydrate, 4 g protein, 5 g fat. **Diabetic Exchanges:** 1 starch, 1 fat.

Golden Au Gratin Potatoes

During the many years I've made this creamy potato dish, I haven't run into anyone who didn't like it! The sauce is very flavorful and just the right consistency.
—Lavonne Hartel
Williston, North Dakota

  1 can (10-3/4 ounces) condensed cream of chicken soup, undiluted
  1 cup (8 ounces) sour cream
3/4 cup butter, melted, *divided*
  3 tablespoons dried minced onion
1/2 teaspoon salt
  1 package (32 ounces) frozen Southern-style hash brown potatoes, thawed
2-1/2 cups shredded cheddar cheese
2-1/2 cups crushed cornflakes

In a large bowl, combine soup, sour cream, 1/2 cup butter, onion and salt. Stir in potatoes and cheese. Transfer to a greased 13-in. x 9-in. x 2-in. baking dish. Toss cornflakes and remaining butter; sprinkle over potatoes.

Bake, uncovered, at 350° for 50-60 minutes or until heated through. **Yield:** 8-10 servings.

Green Chili Rice

With only five ingredients, this rich and creamy rice casserole mixes up in a snap. I always get requests for the recipe.
—Sandra Hanson
Emery, South Dakota

  1 can (10-3/4 ounces) condensed cream of celery soup, undiluted
  1 cup (8 ounces) sour cream
  1 can (4 ounces) chopped green chilies
  1 cup (4 ounces) shredded cheddar cheese
1-1/2 cups uncooked instant rice

In a bowl, combine the soup, sour cream, chilies and cheese. Stir in rice. Transfer to a greased shallow 1-1/2-qt. baking dish. Bake, uncovered, at 350° for 20 minutes or until rice is tender. **Yield:** 4-6 servings.

Carrots Supreme

(Pictured above)

This creamy carrot casserole is always a hit. An easy-to-fix but very special side dish, it goes well with almost any meat or poultry. Even though I serve these dressed-up carrots often, my family still requests them for Christmas dinner.
—Lise Thomson, Magrath, Alberta

  8 cups sliced carrots
  1 small onion, chopped
  1 tablespoon butter
  1 can (10-3/4 ounces) condensed cream of mushroom soup, undiluted
  1 can (4 ounces) mushroom stems and pieces, drained
1/2 cup grated Parmesan cheese
  1 cup soft bread crumbs

Place carrots in a saucepan and cover with water. Bring to a boil. Reduce heat; cover and cook until tender. Meanwhile, in a small skillet, saute onion in butter until tender. Drain carrots; add onion, soup, mushrooms and Parmesan cheese.

Transfer to a greased 2-1/2-qt. baking dish. Sprinkle with bread crumbs. Bake, uncovered, at 350° for 30-35 minutes or until heated through. **Yield:** 8 servings.

Company Potato Casserole

(Pictured below)

Swiss cheese lends distinctive flavor to this rich, creamy potato casserole. Since it tastes wonderful and looks so lovely, this side dish is perfect for serving company or as part of a special holiday meal.
—Mrs. Sylvester Socolovitch
Cheboygan, Michigan

    5 cups cooked cubed peeled potatoes
1-1/2 cups (12 ounces) sour cream
1-1/4 cups shredded Swiss cheese, *divided*
    1/2 cup shredded carrot
    1/4 cup chopped onion
    2 tablespoons minced fresh parsley
    1 teaspoon salt
    1/2 teaspoon dill weed
    1/4 teaspoon pepper
    1/4 teaspoon paprika

In a bowl, combine the potatoes, sour cream, 1 cup cheese, carrot, onion, parsley, salt, dill and pepper. Transfer to a greased 8-in. square baking dish. Sprinkle with the paprika and remaining cheese.

Bake, uncovered, at 350° for 25-35 minutes or until bubbly. **Yield:** 8 servings.

Apple-a-Day Casserole

(Pictured on page 88)

This sweet-tart casserole is a fun change of pace from traditional vegetable side dishes. It's super-quick to prepare if you use a food processor to slice the apples and carrots. The unique combination complements chicken, fish and pork.
—Elizabeth Erwin, Syracuse, New York

    6 medium tart apples, peeled and sliced
    6 medium carrots, thinly sliced
    1/2 cup orange juice
    1/3 cup all-purpose flour
    1/3 cup sugar
    1/2 teaspoon ground nutmeg
    2 tablespoons cold butter

Combine apples and carrots; place in a greased shallow 2-qt. baking dish. Drizzle with orange juice. Cover and bake at 350° for 40-45 minutes or until carrots are crisp-tender.

In a bowl, combine the flour, sugar and nutmeg; cut in butter until crumbly. Sprinkle over apple mixture. Bake, uncovered, 10-15 minutes longer or until the carrots are tender. **Yield:** 6-8 servings.

Cranberry-Apple Butternut Squash

This easy casserole is a wonderful accompaniment for fall and winter dinners. The preserves and marmalade sweeten the cranberries and give the dish a fine fruitiness.
—Pat Waymire
Yellow Springs, Ohio

    2 pounds butternut squash, peeled, seeded and cubed (about 6 cups)
    4 cups water
    1 can (21 ounces) apple pie filling
    3/4 cup whole-berry cranberry sauce
    2 tablespoons orange marmalade
    2 tablespoons apricot preserves

In a large saucepan, combine squash and water; bring to a boil. Reduce heat; cover and simmer until squash is tender, about 25 minutes. Drain.

Spread the pie filling in a greased 8-in. square baking dish. Top with squash. Combine cranberry sauce, marmalade and preserves; spoon over squash. Bake, uncovered, at 350° for 25 minutes or until heated through. **Yield:** 8 servings.

Creamed Onions And Carrots

These can be made ahead of time, which eases pressure on Thanksgiving day. It's one of several side dishes we serve.
—Ardis Rollefson
Jackson Hole, Wyoming

    8 cups water
    2 pounds pearl onions
    2 tablespoons butter
    3 tablespoons all-purpose flour
1-1/4 cups heavy whipping cream
    1/2 teaspoon salt
    1/4 teaspoon pepper
    2 cups shredded carrots

In a Dutch oven or large kettle, bring water to a boil. Add onions; boil for 3 minutes. Drain and rinse in cold water; peel and set aside.

In a large saucepan, melt butter. Stir in flour until smooth. Gradually add cream, salt and pepper. Bring to a boil; cook and stir for 2 minutes or until thickened. Stir in carrots and onions. Transfer to a greased 2-qt. baking dish. Bake, uncovered, at 325° for 30-40 minutes or until vegetables are tender. **Yield:** 12 servings.

Tomato Crouton Casserole

This baked dish uses lots of delicious tomatoes and seasonings that give it an Italian twist.
—Norma Nelson, Punta Gorda, Florida

    8 medium tomatoes, peeled and cut into
        wedges
    8 slices bread, crusts removed and cubed
1/2 cup plus 2 tablespoons butter, melted
    1 teaspoon salt
    1 teaspoon dried basil
    1 teaspoon dried thyme
3/4 cup grated Parmesan cheese

Arrange tomatoes in a greased 13-in. x 9-in. x 2-in. baking dish. Top with bread cubes. Combine butter, salt, basil and thyme; drizzle over bread and tomatoes. Sprinkle with cheese. Bake, uncovered, at 350° for 30-35 minutes or until tomatoes are tender. **Yield:** 8-10 servings.

Bunkhouse Beans

(Pictured above right)

With sliced hot dogs and several types of beans in the mixture, this hearty dish could be a meal in

itself. It was very popular at my son's cowboy theme party. We turned our kitchen peninsula into a "covered wagon" to serve the buffet!
—Sharon Thompson, Oskaloosa, Iowa

    1 cup salsa
    2/3 cup barbecue sauce
    2/3 cup packed brown sugar
    5 hot dogs, halved lengthwise and sliced
    3 tablespoons dried minced onion
    2 cans (16 ounces *each*) pork and beans,
        drained
    1 can (15-1/2 ounces) chili beans,
        undrained
    1 can (15 ounces) butter *or* lima beans,
        rinsed and drained

In a bowl, combine the first five ingredients; mix well. Stir in the beans; pour into an ungreased 2-qt. baking dish. Bake, uncovered, at 375° for 35-40 minutes or until bubbly. **Yield:** 6-8 servings.

Make It Ahead

Many casseroles can be assembled ahead and frozen. Just thaw in the fridge before baking.

Bake 5-10 minutes longer or until the marshmallows just begin to puff and brown. **Yield:** 10-12 servings.

Mexican Corn Casserole

(Pictured below)

This satisfying side dish resembles an old-fashioned spoon bread but with some added zip. My family and friends agree that this recipe really dresses up plain corn. It's a convenient dish to transport to a potluck, too.
—Laura Kadlec
Maiden Rock, Wisconsin

4 eggs
1 can (15-1/4 ounces) whole kernel corn, drained
1 can (14-3/4 ounces) cream-style corn
1-1/2 cups cornmeal
1-1/4 cups buttermilk
1 cup butter, melted
2 cans (4 ounces *each*) chopped green chilies
2 medium onions, chopped
1 teaspoon baking soda
3 cups (12 ounces) shredded cheddar cheese, *divided*
Jalapeno pepper and sweet red pepper rings, optional

Mallow-Topped Sweet Potatoes

(Pictured above)

My grandmother always served this sweet potato casserole at Thanksgiving. The puffy marshmallow topping gives the dish a festive look, and spices enhance the sweet potato flavor. Even those not fond of sweet potatoes love them prepared this way.
—Edna Hoffman, Hebron, Indiana

6 cups hot mashed sweet potatoes (prepared without milk and butter)
1 cup milk
6 tablespoons butter, softened
1/2 cup packed brown sugar
1 egg
1-1/2 teaspoons ground cinnamon
1-1/2 teaspoons vanilla extract
3/4 teaspoon ground allspice
1/2 teaspoon salt
1/4 teaspoon ground nutmeg
18 large marshmallows

In a large mixing bowl, beat the sweet potatoes, milk, butter, brown sugar, egg, cinnamon, vanilla, allspice, salt and nutmeg until smooth.

Transfer to a greased shallow 2-1/2-qt. baking dish. Bake, uncovered, at 325° for 40-45 minutes or until heated through. Top with the marshmallows.

Beat eggs in a large bowl; add the next eight ingredients and mix well. Stir in 2 cups cheese. Pour into a greased 13-in. x 9-in. x 2-in. baking dish. Bake, uncovered, at 325° for 1 hour. Top with remaining cheese. Let stand for 15 minutes before serving. Garnish with peppers if desired. **Yield:** 12-15 servings.

German Potato Casserole

I always bring this potato dish to an annual Oktoberfest party in fall. Everyone likes it, which ensures our invitation back year after year. There are never any leftovers.
—Dara Luburgh
Sparta, New Jersey

  5 pounds red potatoes, peeled and cut
    into 1/2-inch cubes
  1 pound sliced bacon, diced
  8 hard-cooked eggs, chopped
  1 large onion, chopped
  1/2 teaspoon salt
  1/2 teaspoon pepper
1-1/2 cups mayonnaise
  3 tablespoons cider vinegar
  2 tablespoons Worcestershire sauce
  1 pound process cheese (Velveeta), cubed

Place potatoes in a Dutch oven and cover with water. Bring to a boil. Reduce heat; cover and cook for 15-20 minutes or until tender. Drain. In a skillet, cook bacon over medium heat until crisp. Using a slotted spoon, remove to paper towels; drain, reserving 1 tablespoon drippings.

In a large bowl, gently toss the potatoes, bacon, eggs, onion, salt and pepper. Combine the mayonnaise, vinegar, Worcestershire sauce and reserved bacon drippings; add to potato mixture and toss to coat.

Divide half of the mixture between one greased 13-in. x 9-in. x 2-in. baking dish and one 9-in. square baking dish. Top with half of the cheese cubes. Repeat layers. Bake, uncovered, at 350° for 40-45 minutes or until golden brown and bubbly. **Yield:** 16-20 servings.

Editor's Note: Reduced-fat or fat-free mayonnaise is not recommended for this recipe.

Mushroom Green Bean Casserole

(Pictured above right)

Most traditional green bean casseroles center around mushroom soup and french-fried onions.

This from-scratch variation features fresh mushrooms, sliced water chestnuts and slivered almonds.
—Pat Richter, Lake Placid, Florida

  1 pound fresh mushrooms, sliced
  1 large onion, chopped
  1/2 cup butter
  1/4 cup all-purpose flour
  1 cup half-and-half cream
  1 jar (16 ounces) process cheese sauce
  2 teaspoons soy sauce
  1/2 teaspoon pepper
  1/8 teaspoon hot pepper sauce
  1 can (8 ounces) sliced water chestnuts,
    drained
  2 packages (16 ounces *each*) frozen
    French-style green beans, thawed and
    well drained
Slivered almonds

In a skillet, saute mushrooms and onion in butter. Stir in flour until blended. Gradually stir in cream. Bring to a boil; cook and stir for 2 minutes. Stir in the cheese sauce, soy sauce, pepper and hot pepper sauce until cheese is melted. Remove from the heat; stir in water chestnuts.

Place the beans in an ungreased 3-qt. baking dish. Pour the cheese mixture over the top, then sprinkle with the almonds. Bake, uncovered, at 375° for 25-30 minutes or until bubbly. **Yield:** 14-16 servings.

Zucchini Tomato Casserole

(Pictured below)

Even people who don't like zucchini can't seem to get enough of this full-flavored side dish. I always bring it to family gatherings and potlucks because it goes well with any entree. —Cathy Johnston Ranchester, Wyoming

- 6 medium zucchini, diced (about 6 cups)
- 4 tablespoons butter, melted, *divided*
- 2 medium tomatoes, diced
- 1 cup (4 ounces) shredded cheddar cheese
- 1 cup cubed process cheese (Velveeta)
- 1 cup soft bread crumbs
- 2 eggs, beaten
- 2 tablespoons dried minced onion
- 1 tablespoon dried parsley flakes
- 1 teaspoon dried basil
- 1/2 teaspoon garlic powder
- 1/2 teaspoon salt
- 1/2 teaspoon pepper

In a large skillet, saute zucchini in 2 tablespoons butter until crisp-tender; drain well. In a bowl, combine the remaining ingredients. Stir in the zucchini and remaining butter.

Transfer to an ungreased 2-qt. baking dish. Bake, uncovered, at 350° for 25-30 minutes or until bubbly. Let stand for 10 minutes before serving. **Yield:** 8 servings.

Mushroom Wild Rice

This colorful casserole is a standout from my mother's collection of family recipes. Excellent texture and taste guarantee it won't play second fiddle to either the turkey or the pumpkin pie at Thanksgiving! —Charlene Baert, Winnipeg, Manitoba

- 4 cups water
- 1 cup uncooked wild rice
- 1 teaspoon butter
- 1-1/2 teaspoons salt, *divided*
- 1/2 cup uncooked brown rice
- 8 bacon strips, diced
- 2 cups sliced fresh mushrooms
- 1 large onion, chopped
- 1 medium green pepper, chopped
- 1 medium sweet red pepper, chopped
- 1 celery rib, thinly sliced
- 1 can (14-1/2 ounces) beef broth
- 2 tablespoons cornstarch
- 1/4 cup cold water
- 1/2 cup slivered almonds

In a large saucepan, bring water, wild rice, butter and 1/2 teaspoon salt to a boil. Reduce heat; cover and simmer for 40 minutes. Stir in brown rice. Cover and simmer 25-30 minutes longer or until rice is tender.

Meanwhile, in a large skillet, cook bacon until crisp. Remove bacon to paper towels; drain, reserving 2 tablespoons drippings. In the drippings, saute mushrooms, onion, peppers and celery until tender. Stir in broth and remaining salt. Bring to a boil.

In a small bowl, combine the cornstarch and cold water until smooth; stir into the mushroom mixture. Cook and stir for 2 minutes or until thickened and bubbly; stir in almonds and bacon. Drain rice; add mushroom mixture.

Transfer to a greased 13-in. x 9-in. x 2-in. baking dish. Cover and bake at 350° for 25 minutes. Uncover; bake 5-10 minutes longer or until heated through. **Yield:** 12 servings.

Noodles Florentine

With this recipe, you get noodles and a vegetable in one tasty casserole. —Marcia Orlando Boyertown, Pennsylvania

- 5 cups uncooked medium egg noodles
- 2 tablespoons butter
- 2 tablespoons all-purpose flour

1 cup milk
1 package (10 ounces) frozen chopped
    spinach, thawed and well drained
1/4 teaspoon ground nutmeg
Salt and pepper to taste
1 cup (4 ounces) shredded Swiss cheese

In a large saucepan, cook noodles according to package directions until tender. In another saucepan, melt butter; stir in flour until smooth. Gradually add milk. Bring to a boil; cook and stir for 2 minutes or until thickened. Stir in the spinach, nutmeg, salt and pepper. Drain the noodles. Add to spinach mixture; toss gently to coat.

Transfer to a greased shallow 2-qt. baking dish; sprinkle with cheese. Cover; bake at 350° for 20 minutes or until heated through. **Yield:** 4 servings.

Harvest Vegetable Casserole

This recipe brings colorful garden goodness to a large-scale dinner with only minimal preparation.
—Edna Hoffman, Hebron, Indiana

2 large green peppers
1 large sweet red pepper
4 large carrots
4 large tomatoes
3 medium zucchini
1-1/2 pounds green beans
4 large onions, thinly sliced
1/4 cup vegetable oil
1 medium head cauliflower, cut into
    florets
1 package (10 ounces) frozen peas
1 to 2 tablespoons salt
1 tablespoon chicken bouillon granules
3 cups boiling water
1 cup medium pearl barley
3 garlic cloves, minced
1/4 cup lemon juice
2 teaspoons paprika
Minced fresh parsley

Cut peppers, carrots and tomatoes into chunks; cut zucchini and beans into 1-in. pieces. In large skillets, saute onions in oil until tender. Add peppers; cook and stir for 1 minute. Stir in carrots, tomatoes, zucchini, beans, cauliflower and peas. Add salt; stir. In a bowl, dissolve bouillon in water; stir in the barley and garlic.

Transfer to three greased 13-in. x 9-in. x 2-in. baking dishes. Top with vegetable mixture. Drizzle with lemon juice; sprinkle with paprika. Cover and bake at 350° for 1-1/2 hours or until barley and vegetables are tender. Sprinkle with parsley. **Yield:** about 28 (3/4-cup) servings.

Squash Stuffing Casserole

(Pictured above)

Convenient corn bread stuffing mix and a can of green chilies give fast flavor to sliced summer squash. Since I cook for just my husband and me, I often freeze the leftovers for another day.
—Tara Kay Cottingham, Munday, Texas

3/4 cup water
1/4 teaspoon salt
6 cups sliced yellow summer squash (1/4
    inch thick)
1 small onion, halved and sliced
1 can (10-3/4 ounces) condensed cream of
    mushroom soup, undiluted
1 cup (8 ounces) sour cream
1 package (6 ounces) instant corn bread
    stuffing mix
1 can (4 ounces) chopped green chilies
Salt and pepper to taste
1 cup (4 ounces) shredded cheddar
    cheese

In a large saucepan, bring water and salt to a boil. Add squash and onion. Reduce heat; cover and cook until squash is crisp-tender, about 6 minutes. Drain well; set aside. In a bowl, combine soup, sour cream, stuffing and the contents of seasoning packet, chilies, salt and pepper; mix well. Fold in squash mixture.

Pour into a greased shallow 2-qt. baking dish. Sprinkle with cheese. Bake, uncovered, at 350° for 25-30 minutes or until heated through. **Yield:** 8-10 servings.

until crisp-tender. Drain and set aside. In a large skillet, saute onion and garlic in butter until tender. Stir in tomatoes, seasonings, cauliflower and broccoli. Cook, uncovered, until heated through, about 4 minutes, stirring occasionally. Remove from the heat and set aside.

In a large bowl, beat the eggs and cream; stir in 1 cup Swiss cheese, Parmesan cheese and the vegetable mixture. Transfer to a greased shallow 2-qt. baking dish. Sprinkle with the remaining Swiss cheese.

Bake, uncovered, at 375° for 25-30 minutes or until a knife inserted near the center comes out clean. Let stand 10 minutes before serving. **Yield:** 12 servings.

End-of-Summer Vegetable Bake

(Pictured above)

When my husband worked as a deputy ag commissioner, he'd bring me bushels of vegetables from area farms. This pretty side dish is the result—it's easy to fix but impressive enough for company.
—Judy Williams, Hayden, Idaho

   1 small head cauliflower, broken into
     small florets (about 5 cups)
   1 medium bunch broccoli, cut into small
     florets (about 4 cups)
   1 medium onion, chopped
   2 garlic cloves, minced
   1 tablespoon butter
   2 medium tomatoes, chopped
   3/4 teaspoon dried basil
   3/4 teaspoon dried oregano
   3/4 teaspoon salt
   1/4 teaspoon pepper
   1/4 teaspoon hot pepper sauce
   4 eggs
   1/3 cup half-and-half cream
   1-1/2 cups (6 ounces) shredded Swiss
     cheese, *divided*
   1/4 cup shredded Parmesan cheese

Place the cauliflower and broccoli in a saucepan with a small amount of water. Bring to a boil. Reduce heat; cover and simmer for 5-10 minutes or

Nutty Barley Bake

(Pictured below)

When I started bringing this distinctive dish to holiday dinners, a lot of people had never seen barley in anything but soup. They have since dubbed me "the barley lady", and now I wouldn't dare bring anything but this dish. —Renate Crump
Los Angeles, California

   1 medium onion, chopped
   1 cup medium pearl barley
   1/2 cup slivered almonds *or* pine nuts
   1/4 cup butter

1/2 cup minced fresh parsley
1/4 cup thinly sliced green onions
1/4 teaspoon salt
1/8 teaspoon pepper
2 cans (14-1/2 ounces *each*) beef broth
Additional parsley, optional

In a skillet over medium heat, saute the onion, barley and nuts in butter until barley is lightly browned. Stir in the parsley, green onions, salt and pepper.

Transfer to a greased 2-qt. baking dish. Stir in broth. Bake, uncovered, at 350° for 1 hour and 15 minutes or until the barley is tender and the liquid is absorbed. Sprinkle with parsley if desired. **Yield:** 6 servings.

Creamy Sprouts 'n' Noodles

This comforting casserole is great with pork roast or pork chops. It makes a delicious side dish for company. —Dixie Terry, Marion, Illinois

1 pound fresh brussels sprouts, quartered
2 medium onions, finely chopped
4 tablespoons butter, *divided*
1 cup (8 ounces) sour cream
1 cup small-curd cottage cheese
1 garlic clove, minced
1 teaspoon paprika
1/2 teaspoon salt
1/4 to 1/2 teaspoon caraway seeds
3 cups medium egg noodles, cooked and drained
1 cup soft bread crumbs

Place the brussels sprouts and a small amount of water in a saucepan; cover and cook until tender. Meanwhile, in a skillet, saute onions in 2 tablespoons butter until golden brown. Remove from the heat; stir in the sour cream, cottage cheese, garlic, paprika, salt and caraway. Drain sprouts; add to onion mixture with noodles.

Spread into a greased shallow 2-qt. baking dish. Melt remaining butter and toss with bread crumbs. Sprinkle over casserole. Bake, uncovered, at 375° for 20-25 minutes or until golden brown. **Yield:** 6-8 servings.

Festive Green Bean Casserole

(Pictured above right)

This recipe came from a cookbook my son gave to me more than 20 years ago. It's a tasty side dish that I enjoy making often for family get-togethers and potluck suppers. —June Mullins
Livonia, Missouri

1 cup chopped sweet red pepper
1 small onion, finely chopped
1 tablespoon butter
1 can (10-3/4 ounces) condensed cream of celery soup, undiluted
1/2 cup milk
1 teaspoon Worcestershire sauce
1/8 teaspoon hot pepper sauce
2 packages (16 ounces *each*) frozen French-style green beans, thawed and drained
1 can (8 ounces) sliced water chestnuts, drained
1 cup (4 ounces) shredded cheddar cheese

In a skillet, saute red pepper and onion in butter until tender. Add soup, milk, Worcestershire sauce and hot pepper sauce; stir until smooth. Stir in beans and water chestnuts.

Transfer to an ungreased 1-1/2-qt. baking dish. Sprinkle with cheese. Bake, uncovered, at 350° for 15 minutes or until heated through. **Yield:** 6-8 servings.

Carrot Coin Casserole

(Pictured below)

When I started using this comforting casserole recipe over 25 years ago, it was just a creamed vegetable dish. Over time, I've enhanced it by trying different vegetables and adding nutmeg.
—Linda Phillippi, Ronan, Montana

    12 medium carrots, sliced
     1 large onion, cut into 1/4-inch slices
     2 cups frozen peas
 1-1/2 cups (6 ounces) shredded cheddar
         cheese
     4 tablespoons butter, *divided*
     2 tablespoons all-purpose flour
     1 teaspoon salt
   1/4 teaspoon pepper
   1/4 teaspoon ground nutmeg
 2-1/2 cups milk
     1 cup crushed butter-flavored crackers
         (about 25 crackers)

Place carrots and a small amount of water in a saucepan; cover and cook over medium heat until crisp-tender, about 6 minutes. Add onion; bring to a boil. Reduce heat; cover and simmer for 4-6 minutes or until onion is crisp-tender. Drain. Add peas and toss.

Place 4 cups in a greased shallow 3-qt. baking dish; sprinkle with cheese. Top with remaining vegetables. In a saucepan over medium heat, melt 1 tablespoon butter. Stir in flour, salt, pepper and nutmeg until smooth. Gradually add milk, stir-ring constantly. Bring to a boil; boil and stir for 2 minutes. Pour over the vegetables.

In a small saucepan or skillet, combine cracker crumbs and remaining butter; cook and stir over medium heat until toasted. Sprinkle over casserole. Bake, uncovered, at 350° for 30-40 minutes or until bubbly. **Yield:** 12 servings.

Creamy Spinach Bake

When my brother, sisters and I were growing up, Mom knew how to get us to eat our spinach. This casserole has a rich creamy sauce, french-fried onions and a cracker crumb topping. Who can resist? —Debra Falkiner, St. Charles, Missouri

     2 packages (8 ounces *each*) cream
         cheese, softened
     2 cans (10-3/4 ounces *each*) condensed
         cream of mushroom soup, undiluted
     4 packages (10 ounces *each*) frozen
         chopped spinach, thawed and well
         drained
     2 cans (2.8 ounces *each*) french-fried
         onions
   2/3 cup crushed saltines (about 16
         crackers)
   1/4 cup butter, melted

In a bowl, beat the cream cheese until smooth. Add soup; mix well. Stir in spinach and onions. Transfer to a greased 2-1/2-qt. baking dish. Combine cracker crumbs and butter; sprinkle over spinach mixture. Bake, uncovered, at 325° for 30-35 minutes or until heated through. **Yield:** 10 servings.

Scalloped Corn

This comforting casserole features sunny corn kernels tucked into a creamy custard. My mom got this recipe, and many other excellent ones, from her mother. By the time this crowd-pleasing corn dish got around the table, my father, sister, brothers and I would have almost scraped it clean.
—Sandy Jenkins, Elkhorn, Wisconsin

     4 cups fresh *or* frozen corn
     3 eggs, beaten
     1 cup milk
     1 cup crushed saltines (about 30
         crackers), *divided*
     3 tablespoons butter, melted
     1 tablespoon sugar
     1 tablespoon finely chopped onion
Salt and pepper to taste

In a large bowl, combine the corn, eggs, milk, 3/4 cup cracker crumbs, butter, sugar, onion, salt and pepper. Transfer to a greased 1-1/2-qt. baking dish. Sprinkle with remaining cracker crumbs. Bake, uncovered, at 325° for 1 hour or until a knife inserted near the center comes out clean. **Yield:** 6 servings.

Two-Bean Tomato Bake

Parmesan cheese, basil and garlic spice up this mouth-watering medley of beans, mushrooms, onion and tomato. A crumb topping adds crunch to this veggie bake that's even more flavorful when you use your garden harvest. —Dorothy Rieke
Julian, Nebraska

1-1/2 pounds fresh green beans, cut
    into 2-inch pieces
1-1/2 pounds fresh wax beans, cut
    into 2-inch pieces
   5 medium tomatoes, peeled and cubed
  1/2 pound fresh mushrooms, sliced
   1 medium sweet onion, chopped
  10 tablespoons butter, *divided*
1-1/2 teaspoons minced garlic, *divided*
1-1/2 teaspoons dried basil, *divided*
1-1/2 teaspoons dried oregano, *divided*
   1 teaspoon salt
1-1/2 cups soft bread crumbs
  1/3 cup grated Parmesan cheese

Place beans in a large saucepan and cover with water; bring to a boil. Cook, uncovered, for 8-10 minutes or until crisp-tender. Drain; add the tomatoes and set aside.

In a skillet, saute mushrooms and onion in 4 tablespoons butter. Add 1 teaspoon garlic, 1 teaspoon basil, 1 teaspoon oregano and salt. Add to the bean mixture; toss to coat. Spoon into a greased 3-qt. baking dish.

Melt the remaining butter; toss with bread crumbs, Parmesan cheese and remaining garlic, basil and oregano. Sprinkle over bean mixture. Cover and bake at 400° for 20 minutes. Uncover; bake 15 minutes longer or until golden brown. **Yield:** 14-16 servings.

Parmesan Onion Bake

(Pictured above right)

Dinner guests in my home know to expect the unexpected! I love experimenting with unusual combinations of ingredients. This cheesy onion bake adds flair to a meal. —Linda Vail, Ballwin, Missouri

   6 medium onions, sliced
   1 cup diced celery
   8 tablespoons butter, *divided*
  1/4 cup all-purpose flour
   1 teaspoon salt
  1/8 teaspoon pepper
1-1/2 cups milk
  1/3 cup grated Parmesan cheese
  1/2 cup chopped pecans

In a skillet, saute onions and celery in 3 tablespoons butter until tender; drain and set aside. In a saucepan, melt remaining butter; stir in flour, salt and pepper until smooth. Gradually stir in milk. Bring to a boil; cook and stir for 2 minutes or until thickened. Pour over vegetables; toss to coat.

Pour into an ungreased 2-qt. baking dish. Sprinkle with cheese and pecans. Bake, uncovered, at 350° for 20-25 minutes or until heated through. **Yield:** 6-8 servings.

Make It Au Gratin!

Turn any casserole into an au gratin dish by sprinkling with a topping of bread crumbs and grated cheese; butter may also be dotted over the top. After the dish is baked, the topping will be crisp and golden brown.

General Recipe Index

✓ Recipe includes Nutritional Analysis and Diabetic Exchanges

✓ Recipe includes Nutritional Analysis and Diabetic Exchanges

✓ Recipe includes Nutritional Analysis and Diabetic Exchanges

✓ Recipe includes Nutritional Analysis and Diabetic Exchanges

✓ Recipe includes Nutritional Analysis and Diabetic Exchanges